CAMARO & FIREBIRD PERFORMANCE HANDBOOK

Peter C. Sessler

Motorbooks International
Publishers & Wholesalers ®

First published in 1993 by Motorbooks International
Publishers & Wholesalers, PO Box 2, 729 Prospect Avenue,
Osceola, WI 54020 USA

Motorbooks International books are also available at
discounts in bulk quantity for industrial or sales-
promotional use. For details write to Special Sales
Manager at the Publisher's address

Library of Congress Cataloging-in-Publication Data
Sessler, Peter C.
    Camaro & Firebird performance handbook / Peter C.
Sessler.
        p.   cm. — (Motorbooks performance handbook
series)
    Includes index.
    ISBN 0-87938-711-4
    1. Camaro automobile—Performance—Amateurs'
manuals.   2. Camaro automobile—Maintenance and
repair—Amateurs' manuals.   3. Firebird automobile—
Performance—Amateurs' manuals.   4. Firebird
automobile—Maintenance and repair—Amateurs'
manuals.   I. Title.   II. Title: Camaro and Firebird
performance handbook.   III. Series.
TL215.C33S48   1993
629.222'2—dc20   92-33695

On the front cover: A 1991 Camaro Z-28. Vehicle courtesy
Fox Chevrolet, Baltimore, Maryland. *Nick Nicaise*

On the back cover: A 1985 Camaro IROC-Z, *Chevrolet
Motor Div.*; a 1991 Firebird Trans Am convertible, *Pontiac
Motor Div.*; rod end caps are installed during an engine
rebuild; the restrictive stock air cleaner of a 305ci engine
will be changed for better breathing.

Printed and bound in the United States of America

Contents

Acknowledgments

I would like to thank all those who have assisted me in writing this book by generously contributing their time, information, and help. Special thanks to Steve Collison, Bill Haenelt, Bob Pelc, Quality Engine Distributors, and General Motors Corporation's Chevrolet and Pontiac Motor Divisions.

All photos were provided by the author except where indicated.

Introduction

Third-generation Camaros and Firebirds have been with us since 1982, when the reengineered F-body platform, on which both are based finally superseded the second-generation cars. The third-generation F-bodies closely follow the size and concept of the original 1967 models—which has ensured their success and acceptance. Leaner and trimmer, the Camaro and Firebird provide transportation with style and flair and offer a high level of performance.

Since their introduction in 1966, the Camaro and Firebird have portrayed a youthful image. For Detroit in the 1960s, a youthful image meant a car that was stylish, smaller than what parents drove, a car that performed better (or at least *felt* that way) and, of course, it had to be affordable. The original Camaro and Firebird did all these things. Youth also meant performance and from the start, the Camaro could be optionally equipped with versions of Chevrolet's big-block V-8 and the Firebird with Pontiac's 400ci (cubic inch) big-block.

Not to be outdone, Chevrolet also introduced the Z-28 Camaro in 1967 for those enthusiasts who wanted good handling along with acceleration. From the start, the Camaro and Firebird quickly established themselves as the performance pony cars to have, easily overtaking the Mustang, at least in the performance sphere.

The Camaro models synonymous with performance were those equipped with the Super Sport (SS) option package. Besides the usual graphics, this meant a firmer suspension and larger engine. These cars were equipped with a version of the popular Chevrolet small-block V-8 while the larger 396ci big-block was the choice of those favoring straight-line acceleration. While making an inauspicious start in 1967, the Z-28 Camaro quickly set the pace as well—and created the image—for what an all-around performance pony car should be in the late 1960s.

Although the first-generation Firebirds didn't sell as well as the Camaro, their performance potential was equal to the Camaro. Firebirds equipped with one of the Ram Air 400 engines offered blistering acceleration. Pontiac did not have a suitable small-block V-8 engine to counter the successful Z-28 Camaro. Yet in 1969, Pontiac quietly introduced the Trans Am Firebird which was able to provide excellent handling with a big-block V-8 engine. In the years to come, the Trans Am set the standard for Detroit performance sedans.

The Camaro and Firebird were restyled in 1970, but basically little was changed from the first-generation 1967 models. The big-block V-8 engine and SS option package continued to be available on the Camaro only until 1972, but it was becoming clear that the true performance Camaro was the Z-28. With a larger version of the small-block V-8, the Z-28 offered big-block acceleration without the weight

4

penalty of the bigger engine, with better handling to boot. The Z-28 remained the premier performance Camaro through the 1970s, though it was not offered during 1975–76. After 1973, increased emphasis was place on handling and correspondingly less on horsepower, at least from Chevrolet. With the demise of the big-block engines, most Camaros were powered by versions of the Chevrolet small-block.

While Chevrolet deemphasized performance, Pontiac bucked the trend and continued to offer high-performance models and engines until 1974. The premier performance model was the Trans Am, with the Formula model following close behind. The largest Pontiac V-8, displacing 455ci, was offered until 1975 and the 400ci Pontiac V-8 until 1978. The Oldsmobile 403ci V-8 gradually displaced the Pontiac V-8 by 1979. During this period, the Firebird Trans Am established itself as the premier American performance car. By the early 1980s, though, it was becoming apparent that the Camaro and Firebird were just too large and heavy. Actually, it was amazing that they remained popular as long as they did.

The third-generation F-body Camaro and Firebird made their debut in 1982. The basic body shell and suspension design has remained consistent since then, although it has been constantly refined through the years. Rather than breaking with the past, the high-performance models have been the same—the Z-28 Camaro and the Trans Am Firebird. Unlike the previous-generation cars, both the Camaro and Firebird have shared the same engines (except the 1989 Twenty-fifth Anniversary Edition Trans Am) which for the performance enthusiast has meant the small-block Chevrolet V-8. It is this engine that General Motors decided to upgrade for the 1980s.

Finally, the current fourth-generation Camaro and Firebird made their appearance in early 1993. Both cars have been dramatically restyled, yet they retained the previous 101.1in wheelbase and general proportions. Both cars received major chassis and mechanical changes that have addressed most of the shortcomings of the third-generation cars, resulting in a fresh, contemporary package.

Only one engine has been common to all Camaros produced to date and Firebirds since 1982: the Chevrolet small-block V-8. Introduced in 1955, the small-block was Chevrolet's first V-8 since 1917. It has since set the standard for performance V-8s because of its well-engineered design and horsepower potential. The sheer number of them produced, over sixty million, has made the engine a favorite among hot rodders and racers alike. It has been, and still is by far, GM's most popular street engine. The small-block has been the recipient of extensive factory experimentation and a wealth of factory performance parts.

In the 1970s, low-horsepower versions of the small-block were as much as the enthusiast was going to get from Chevrolet as original equipment, but the aftermarket industry helped to remedy that situation.

The manufacturer horsepower wars started again in earnest in 1982 when the redesigned third-generation Camaro and Firebird became available with injected 305ci Chevy small-blocks. Partly to counter the resurrected Mustang GT, the new F-body also needed more power to remain competitive. By 1987, a 350ci version was optionally available.

On the current fourth-generation cars, the venerable small-block carries the LT1 designation—first used in 1970—which is synonymous with power and high performance. Boasting several improvements, the LT1 5.7 liter is rated at 275hp, 30hp more than the 1992 5.7 liter, and it has the potential for a lot more.

Since their inception, the Camaro and Firebird have always provided the enthusiast with a solid foundation on which to build. Underneath the skin, the third-generation and current cars differ from the first two in two areas. The third-generation cars use a MacPherson strut front suspension and a coil spring rear—these don't present much of a problem for suspension modifications. The second area involves fuel injection and electronics. When you get down to it, modifying the 305/350ci engine for more power is a fairly standard procedure. Most of the combinations were worked out years ago. However, the big difference today is that all of GM's engines are computer controlled and in order to meet the ever tighter emission requirements, fuel injection has replaced carburetors. Thus the hot rodder has been forced to reeducate himself or herself.

Camaro/Firebird Performance Handbook explores all the current avenues available to those wishing to extract more performance from their third-generation pony cars—from engine swaps to supercharging to even better handling and braking. An effort has been made to keep everything on a realistic level. After all, for many owners, their Camaro or Firebird is their only means of transportation and they may have to cope with the realities of a limited budget. Still, those who must have the latest innovations no matter what the cost, such as a set of $6,000 cylinder four-valve heads, aren't forgotten.

Take note of one final point. In late 1990, a new set of Clean Air Amendments were approved. The Environmental Protection Agency (EPA) sent a policy letter to automotive parts manufacturers, distributors, retailers, and installers stating that the EPA believes the new regulations prohibit "any person from manufacturing, selling, offering for sale, or installing any part or component intended for use with, or as a part of any motor vehicle, where a principal effect of the part or component is to bypass, defeat or render inoperative any emission control device or element of design and where the person knows or should know the part or component is being put to such use. A civil penalty of up to $2500.00 may be imposed for each violation of this defeat device prohibition."

Except for California, which had already prohibited the car owner from tampering with emissions equipment, there hadn't been a federal mandate declaring the same thing. No longer can the "Not for sale or use in California of pollution controlled motor vehicles" disclaimer be used on the rest of the forty-nine states.

Still, the law is ambiguous on what constitutes a "defeat device." If the law is strictly interpreted it would mean that you can't make any modifications to a street car and if you wanted to turn your Camaro or Firebird into a racer, well, you couldn't do that either. Until the guidelines are made clear, you shouldn't tamper with or disable any of your engine's emission devices. This means don't disconnect the exhaust gas recirculation (EGR) system or take the catalytic converters off. But it doesn't mean you can't replace the stock catalytic converters with aftermarket units that flow a lot better. You don't have to be a genius to know that future guidelines will prohibit any disabling of emission control systems.

Things aren't as bad as they sound, however. There are many parts that, while they can affect the engine's emissions output, won't disable the stock emission control systems, such as a more radical camshaft, headers, intake manifolds, superchargers, or freer-flowing cylinder heads. In the past, when such parts were sold in California, the California Air Resources Board (CARB) certified them acceptable for sale as long as they passed tests showing that they did not increase emissions. It seems likely that the EPA will go along with such procedures, too.

More performance parts are being certified. For example, the Paxton supercharger has been certified as acceptable. The reality is, with technology being what it is today, you can build a high-horsepower engine and still meet current emission standards. The outcome of all this will be clean-running performance engines, and when you think about it, there is no reason why it shouldn't be that way.

Chapter 1

Camaro/Firebird Performance History

Look at the Camaro and Firebird and you'll find that their history is steeped in performance. There were always performance Camaro and Firebird models offered. Sometimes they didn't perform very well, such as the mid-1970 to early 1980 models, but that was the case for most American manufacturers at the time. Still, even when high performance wasn't much of a priority at GM, you'll find that both of these cars never lost their performance image.

Along with their obvious sporty styling and flair, their engines made them the performers they were and are today. We'll now take a look at the great engines that have powered these cars.

1967–69

The Camaro was a high-performance pony car, provided it was optioned accordingly, from its inception. During the 1960s all the high-performance

Chevrolet models, whether they were Chevelles, Novas, or Impalas, were designated Super Sport models. So when the Camaro was introduced, it was available as a Super Sport. The convertible or coupe also could be optioned as such, and besides receiving the unique SS identification of striping and oil cooler hood louvers, Super Sport Camaros came with the F41 heavy-duty suspension, dual exhausts, and a choice of engines, with the 396ci big-block topping the list. Naturally, the hot street performers were those equipped with the 396. From 1967–69, the 396ci was available in three variations. In 1967, the 396 V-8 was available in 325 and 375hp (horsepower) forms. The L35 325hp 396 came with a Quadrajet carburetor, hydraulic camshaft, and the regular small-port cylinder heads. The L78 375hp version came with a solid lifter camshaft, big-port big-valve cylinder heads, and a Holley carburetor. In 1968, the L34 350hp version

The Camaro at its purest—this is a 1967 Z-28 powered by the highly tuned 302ci small-block. Note lack of any Z-28 *identification. Most first-generation Camaros were powered by a version of the Chevrolet small-block V-8.*

was added to the option list. Also in 1968, the 375hp 396 was available with aluminum cylinder heads. However, you'll find that the great majority of Camaros were equipped with 307, 327, and 350ci small-block V-8s.

Still, there was a budding market for those who appreciated other performance qualities as well, such as good cornering and braking. In order to qualify for the Sports Car Club of America's (SCCA) Trans-Am series, Chevrolet introduced the Z-28 Camaro in 1967.

Rather than relying on brute torque, the Z-28 was powered by a highly tuned, high-winding version of the Chevrolet small-block V-8, displacing 302ci and pumping out 290hp. Combining acceleration with excellent handling, the Z-28 quickly caught on, forcing other manufacturers to come out with equivalent cars, most notably Ford's Boss 302 Mustang in 1969.

Only 602 Z-28s were built in 1967; by 1969, 20,302 were produced. In keeping with its image, dual four-barrel carburetion was optional on the 302, and for the suspension, four-wheel disc brakes were optional as well. The 1968 Camaro was essentially the same car, and it got a facelift for 1969. The performance powertrains were basically unchanged, but for many enthusiasts, the few 1969 COPO (Central Office Production Order) Camaros built represent the ultimate performance Camaros. Although they were never officially available, they were specially ordered by dealers. What made them unique is that they were powered by 425hp 427ci versions of the Chevrolet big-block. COPO 9561 Camaros were equipped with a cast-iron 427ci V-8 while COPO 9560 cars had aluminum-block 427s. Only sixty-nine of the aluminum-block-equipped Camaros were built. As it turned out, 1969 was the highpoint for 1960s style performance Camaros.

As the Pontiac Firebird shared the same body shell, suspension, and driveline with the Camaro, it differed in styling and in motivating power. High-performance Firebirds were powered by the 400ci Pontiac V-8. The top performance engines were known as the Ram Air series, and except for some minor detail differences, they were the same engines that powered the Pontiac GTO.

In 1969, the Camaro was restyled for a more aggressive, performance look. By this time, the Z-28 option had really caught on.

One of the most visible Camaros built was the 1969 Indy Pace Car Edition, with its white exterior and orange interior. Other Indy Pace Car Camaros were built in 1967, 1982, and again in 1992. Chevrolet Motor Div.

The most significant Firebird in this period was the 1969 Trans Am model. Powered by the 400ci V-8, increased emphasis was placed on handling as it came with front and rear antisway bars, power steering, and power disc brakes. Even though the Pontiac V-8 was heavy, careful suspension tuning made the Trans Am a great-handling car for its time.

On the racetrack, the Z-28 Camaro got most of the attention. In SCCA's Trans-Am road race series, Z-28 Camaros prepared by Roger Penske and driven by Mark Donohue won the series in 1968–69, humbling Ford's Mustang in a classic Ford vs. Chevy confrontation. What made the Camaro victories more impressive was the fact that the Ford operation was a full-fledged factory effort while, at best, the Penske effort was a Chevrolet back-door operation. On the drag strip, big- and small-block-powered Camaros quickly caught on as they were the ideal vehicle in many classes. The Firebird, on the other hand, did not fare as well on the track since it did not have the same popularity. Several Firebirds were raced in the Trans-Am series, but these used Chevrolet small-block engines because Pontiac did not have an acceptable 305ci small-block engine.

1970–81

The Camaro and Firebird were extensively restyled in 1970, but beneath the skin, the cars were essentially unchanged. Although the second-generation F-body lasted until 1981 with only minor styling changes, both cars' popularity increased during the 1970s. These were the only two that stayed with the original pony car concept—the Mustang was downsized while all the other pony cars were dropped. By 1977, the Camaro finally outsold the Mustang.

The Super Sport Camaros continued on only until 1972 when the Super Sport option was finally dropped. The big-block 396ci engine was also deleted from the options list. Big-block Camaros were no longer selling as well as they did because the Z-28 Camaro was a much better car. For 1970, the high-winding 302ci V-8 was replaced by a 360hp version of the 350 small-block, essentially the same as the Corvette LT1 engine. Less weight up front meant better balance and handling, and in terms of acceleration, the Z-28 was quicker. With its larger 15x7in wheels and F60x15in tires, it was able to put more power on the road than the Super Sport Camaros. The solid lifter 350 continued on until 1972 rated at 255hp, but in 1973, a hydraulic camshaft enabled the Z-28 to be equipped with air conditioning for the first time.

The Camaro got a facelift in 1974, resulting in the basic look that continued until 1981. The 350ci small-block was the largest engine available, but as the decade wore on, horsepower ratings declined to the 155–165 range for the optional 350 V-8. In 1980 the optional LM1 350ci (standard with the Z-28) was rated at 190hp, but dropped down to 175hp for 1981. Clearly, the emphasis on performance was downgraded at Chevrolet, and there wasn't even a Z-28 model available in 1975–76.

While Chevrolet shied away from its performance past, Pontiac took a different course. For 1970, it was still business as usual regarding high performance. The Trans Am was joined by a new Firebird model, the Formula—a more economical high-performance Firebird. The Ram Air III and IV 400ci V-8s were the top engine options, 335 and 345hp respectively, but in addition the Trans Am took a giant step forward in the handling department. In 1971, the Trans Am got the 455 High Output (HO) engine as

The second-generation 1970 Camaro—a classic design if there ever was one. The same basic design would continue through 1981. Chevrolet Motor Div.

standard equipment, rated at 335hp. The same engine was carried over into 1972, but with a lower horsepower rating.

By 1973, it was only Pontiac that still offered a true high-performance big-block V-8. This was the

The familiar SS emblem stood for Super Sport. These Camaros were certainly super, especially the big-block-powered versions such as this 1970 375hp 396. Its forte was straight-line acceleration. The year 1972 would be the last year for the big-block Camaros.

455 Super Duty (SD) rated at 310hp (early) and 290hp (late). It came with a special reinforced four-bolt main cylinder block with cylinder heads that featured revised round ports and forged steel connecting rods. It was optional on the Formula and Trans Am Firebirds. Although not many were sold, the 455 SD was carried over into 1974 as well.

Even though the 455ci V-8 was initially dropped for 1975, it was brought back and continued on until the 1976 model year. Labeled the 455 HO, it put out only 200hp, quite anemic by earlier standards. Even so, the Trans Am's image remained that of a high-performance pony car. This was accentuated by the Limited Edition models that started to appear in 1976. These were specially trimmed Trans Ams—black paint with gold trim and accents. Through the rest of the 1970s, Special and Limited Edition Trans Ams were brought out every year.

In terms of engines, the Pontiac 400 V-8 continued on until 1979, but the Oldsmobile-built 403ci V-8 had been available on certain Firebird models since 1977. They weren't high-performance engines by any means, strangled with restrictive catalytic single-exhaust systems, but Pontiac did try and succeeded in upgrading the Firebird's suspension. In 1979, part

Continual refinement made the Camaro a better car as the 1970s rolled on. In 1979, a new Camaro joined the line-up—the Berlinetta, which emphasized luxury. Chevrolet Motor Div.

The 1982 Camaro was an instant hit. Its beautiful styling and fantastic handling made it the car of choice for the performance enthusiast. Once again, it was chosen to pace the prestigious Indy 500 race. Chevrolet Motor Div.

A convertible joined the line-up in 1987—this is the 1992 RS convertible with the Heritage Appearance Package. The 1990s aerodynamic styling is combined with early Z-28 striping. Chevrolet Motor Div.

In 1985 the IROC-Z performance Camaro became avail-
able. The IROC series featured identically equipped
Camaros raced by the world's best drivers. Chevrolet
Motor Div.

While the Camaro took most of the limelight Pontiac's
version of the F-body, the Firebird, proved to be a
formidable performer, especially with the 400ci engine.
Pontiac Motor Div.

of the optional WS6 Special Performance package included rear disc brakes.

While the 1980–81 Camaro could still be equipped with the Chevy small-block displacing 350ci, Pontiac's largest engine was the 301ci V-8. To make up for the lack of cubic inches, a 210hp turbocharged version was available on the Formula and Trans Am.

An interesting phenomenon occurred on the Firebird, which had a tendency to dilute the car's Pontiac image. Besides the 403ci Oldsmobile engine that became available on the Formula and Trans Am, other GM engines soon found their way into the Firebird's engine compartment. This included the Oldsmobile 350 V-8, the Buick 231 V-6 and 350 V-8, and the Chevrolet small-block V-8.

1982–92

By this time, it was clear that the F-body was no longer the right car for the 1980s. The same basic body shell that had been around since 1970 seemed bloated compared to the smaller, trimmer cars that Detroit was building. Also, the redesigned 1979 Mustang was selling well.

The third-generation F-body cars were finally introduced in 1982. These were totally new, yet in size and concept they bore great resemblance to the original 1967 models. Built on a shorter 101in wheel-base they did not use a front subframe, as had the previous two generations, but were a full unit-body construction. In the rear, coil springs replaced the leaf springs, and in the front, modified MacPherson struts were used. Initially, only a two-door coupe hatchback was available, but the Camaro got a convertible in 1987, with the Firebird following in 1991.

Unlike the previous generation, both the Camaro and Firebird shared identical engines and drivetrains. The only exception was the 1989 Twentieth Anniversary Edition Trans Am which came with the 245hp Buick turbocharged 3.8 liter V-6. To date, this is the fastest stock F-body, capable of low 13sec (second) quarter-mile times.

From 1982 to 1986 the standard engine on both was a Pontiac 2.5 liter four-cylinder engine. A Chevrolet 2.8 liter V-6 was optional. In 1987 the four-cylinder was dropped, with the 2.8 liter V-6 becoming the standard engine. It, too, was replaced in 1990 with an improved 3.1 liter V-6. Both the four-cylinder and V-6 were somewhat lacking when it came to horsepower, though. Standard on the Trans Am and Z-28 in 1982 was a carbureted 145hp version of the small-block V-8. The 165hp dual throttle body (cross-fire) injected engine was optional. Both V-8s displaced 5.0 liters (305ci).

The Crossfire V-8 lasted only until 1983 when it was replaced by another carbureted version of the

It was the Firebird Trans Am model that really made an impact on the street scene. Big engines, great handling, *and attractive styling made the Trans Am the performance car of choice in the 1970s. Pontiac Motor Div.*

Incredibly, Pontiac was still offering big-block power in the Trans Am and Formula models until 1979. This is a 1979.

In the 1980s, the Trans Am continued to provide enthusiasts with a distinctive performance package. Pontiac Motor Div.

small-block, rated at 190hp. By 1985, an improved fuel injection system, the Tuned Port Injection (TPI) system replaced carburetors on the optional high-output engines. And in 1987, a 5.7 liter (350ci) small-block became optional as well. Bigger, more powerful engines became necessary because the horsepower wars were once again in full swing. The Camaro and Firebird were enjoying renewed acceptance among enthusiasts—it was a matter of keeping up with the competition.

Besides larger engines, the third-generation Camaro and Firebird have benefited from considerably improved suspension systems. Larger front and rear antisway bars along with wider, lower profile tires have become the norm. Sixteen-inch wheels were first seen on 1984 Fifteenth Anniversary Edition Trans Ams and in 1985 on the International Race of Champions (IROC) optioned Z-28s. Along with optional four-wheel disc brakes, the third-generation Camaro and Firebird are among the world's best-handling cars.

In keeping with their high-performance heritage, the fourth-generation cars got a dose of extra horsepower on the Z-28 and Trans Am in the form of the LT1 5.7 liter V-8 in addition to an improved suspension and a six-speed manual transmission. Even the base Camaro and Firebird owner has benefitted as the standard 3.4 liter V-6 engine is rated at 160hp—almost the same horsepower that the early third-generation cars offered with the optional 5.0 liter V-8.

On the track, Camaros and Firebirds raced in SCCA's Showroom Stock series and the International Motorsports Association's (IMSA) Firehawk and Bridgestone series. Although these cars aren't as heavily modified as the older Trans Am models and competition is very keen, the F-body cars have done very well, winning these series frequently in the past few years. The Camaros and Firebirds raced in the Trans Am series may outwardly resemble stock cars, but in reality they are all-out race cars.

Firebirds have always been distinctive when it comes to styling. The 1991 Trans Am convertible is no different. Pontiac Motor Div.

The small-block Chevrolet V-8 has been with us since 1955. An excellent design back then, the small-block has shown its staying power and adaptability. Clearly, it is the best American V-8 engine. Chevrolet Motor Div.

The current-generation F-body cars are once again enjoying great grass-roots success on the drag strip. Offering an excellent power-to-weight ratio and a considerable amount of support from the factory and the aftermarket, they are a favorite among drag racers. And because they are such good-handling cars, you'll often see them on the autocross circuit.

Chevrolet Small-Block V-8 History

When you look at American performance engines, you'll find that only one has established itself as the standard by which all others are judged. That, of course, is the Chevrolet small-block V-8 which first came into production in 1955. In its original form, the small-block was an engineering work of art. At only 575lb, it was a simple design that was economical to manufacture and proved to be an easy-revving, smooth-running engine. Its best features included a forged steel crankshaft, interchangeable left-to-right cylinder heads, and a light, yet strong valvetrain that featured hollow pushrods and stud-mounted stamped-steel rocker arms. All this and it was reliable.

In its original form, the small-block displaced 265ci. By 1957, displacement went up to 283ci and along with numerous internal improvements, was made into an even better engine. Multiple carburetion systems were responsible for increasingly higher horsepower output, but more significant was the addition of the Rochester Ram Jet constant-flow fuel injection system, in 1957. Fuel injected 283s were optional on the Impala and on the Corvette and continued to be available (only on the Corvette) until 1965.

Fuel injection isn't new on the small-block. A mechanical Rochester Ram Jet fuel injection system was optional in 1957 and continued on until 1965 on Corvettes. Chevrolet Motor Div.

A high point in small-block development was the 1967–69 302ci Z-28 motor which was conservatively rated at 290hp. A high-lift mechanical lifter camshaft, high-rise intake manifold, and Holley four-barrel carburetor combined to make the small-block a high-revving screamer. Chevrolet Motor Div.

As cars got larger and heavier, the small-block's bore and stroke were increased to 4.00x3.25in in 1962, resulting in 327ci. In its highest output, a Corvette fuel injected 327 pumped out 375hp in 1965. Production of the 327 engine ended in 1969. By increasing the stroke to 3.48in, the 327 grew to 350ci in 1967, and it is still in production today. A significant improvement made on the 350 was the use of four-bolt main caps on the center three caps. This applied to the higher performance versions and certain truck blocks.

Besides the changes made to the small-block's bore and stroke over the years, the only other major internal change occurred in 1968. From its introduction in 1955, the small-block had 2.30in diameter main bearing journals with 2.00in diameter rod journals. In 1968 these dimensions were changed to 2.45x2.10in.

The largest production displacement was reached in 1970, with 400ci. Using a 4.125in bore and 3.75in stroke, the cylinders are siamesed with no coolant circulation. Engine cooling is borderline with this engine, particularly if it has been modified. The 400ci blocks can be identified by the freeze plugs on each side of the block. From 1970–77, the 400ci blocks

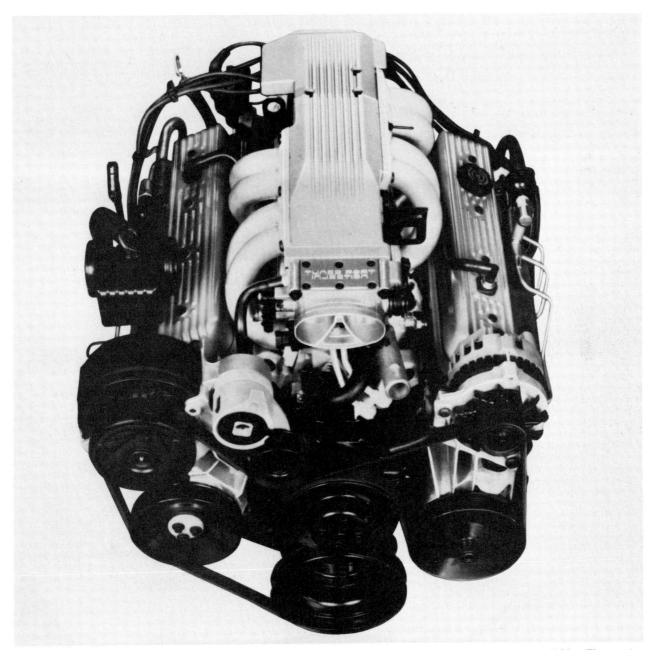

Through the use of a highly sophisticated electronic Tuned Port Injection (TPI) system, the small-block has suc- *cessfully made the transition to the 1980s. Electronics have made the small-block even better. Chevrolet Motor Div.*

*Big-block Camaros weren't around for long—only from
1967–72—but their performance reputation is legend-
ary. This is a 1967 375hp 396.*

*The ultimate Z-28 302ci V-8 came with dual 600cfm
(cubic feet per minute) four-barrel carburetors on a
special manifold in 1969.*

Go to a drag strip today and you'll still see plenty of first-generation Camaros.

Mark Donohue in the Sunoco Camaro. Camaros have been extremely successful in road racing, winning the Trans-Am series in 1968–69. SCCA

were built with four-bolt main caps. By 1978, two-bolt mains were used. Production ended in 1980.

The small-block has also been available in other displacements as well: 267, 302, 305, and 307ci have been used in various applications. Of these, it is the 302 that is one of the high points in the history of the small-block. Available only during 1967–69, it was the original Z-28 engine. It featured a solid lifter camshaft, aluminum high-rise intake manifold with a Holley carburetor, and put out 290hp. Actual output, however, was closer to 350. Another highpoint is the 1970 LT1. Similar in concept to the 302, the LT1 put out 370hp in Corvettes and 360hp in 1970 Camaros.

The current crop of small-blocks has made the transition to the 1980s and 1990s quite well. The use of electronic fuel injection (EFI) systems and computer controls has enabled Chevrolet engineers to extract considerable power while maintaining better than ever driveability and legal emissions output.

About the only problem that seems common to most small-blocks is the oil leakage around the valve covers, which can be aggravated by overtightened

Firebirds, too, raced in the original Trans-Am series. This is Jerry Titus in a 1970 Trans Am Firebird. SCCA

Camaros won the Trans-Am championship in 1991. Here, Scott Sharp is driving the winning Team Duracell Camaro. Unlike the earlier Trans-Am Camaros, today's

Trans-Am racers bear little resemblance to production cars. Mark Weber/Firestone

In the Firestone Firehawk series, only minor modifications are allowed on production cars. This makes for extremely close racing and as you'd expect, the F-body cars are regularly well represented at the finish line. Dennis Ashlock/Firestone

The 1993 model represents the fourth time the Camaro has undergone a major styling and chassis transformation. Sharing the same wheelbase as the third-generation cars, the 1993 Camaro is slightly longer, wider, and taller. The roof, doors, hatch, and spoiler are made of a sheet molded compound (SMC)—a fiberglass and resin mixture. The front fenders and fascia are made of reaction-molded polyurea reinforced with mica. Only the hood and rear fenders are made of steel. Chevrolet Motor Div.

valve cover bolts. The rear main seal can also be a source of leaks. Originally the seal was a rope type, but this was changed to a two-piece rubber seal. Beginning with 1987, major revisions were made to improve sealing. The cylinder head valve cover gasket surface was increased in height and the valve covers themselves were thicker and used an inner oil shield to protect the silicone rubber gaskets. The valve covers are fastened to the cylinder head differently as well, using four long bolts that pass through the center of the covers.

As for the rear main seal, a one-piece unit replaced the two-piece seal. The crankshaft flywheel flange was removed and the rear of the case was faced off to accept a cast-aluminum retainer that is bolted on and holds the seal in place. Oil pan sealing was also improved with increased side reinforcement and now uses a one-piece silicone gasket for sealing.

Probably the most unusual change to the small-block has been the use of a roller lifter hydraulic camshaft which has required additional block machining at the factory. The results in increased output, though, are worth it.

The latest incarnation of the small-block is once again designated LT1. Originally installed in 1992, the Corvette 350ci engine features a reverse-flow cooling system with a gear-driven water pump and a front-mounted optical distributor, and it comes from Chevrolet filled with synthetic motor oil. Cylinder heads are made of aluminum and the compression ratio is 10.25:1, and the result is up to a 300hp output. The LT1 used on the 1993 "F" body cars is rated at 275hp.

Few engines have lasted as long as the Chevrolet small-block. The engine has consistently proven its superiority on the track and on the street and because of its inherently good design and flexibility, it will be around for a long time to come. It certainly has passed the test of time!

Beneath the skin, the 1993 Camaro and Firebird share the same mechanicals and configuration. One departure from the third-generation cars is the use of short and long arm front suspension rather than struts. Chevrolet Motor Div.

Small-Block Chevrolet V-8 Engine and Crank Specifications

CID (ci)	Year	Bore (in)	Stroke (in)	Rod/Main Journals (in)	CID (ci)	Year	Bore (in)	Stroke (in)	Rod/Main Journals (in)
						Present			
262	1974–76	3.671	3.100	2.10/2.45	307	1968–73	3.875	3.250	2.10/2.45
265	1955–57	3.50	3.00	2.00/2.30	327	1962–67	4.00	3.25	2.00/2.30
267	1979–82	3.50	3.48	2.10/2.45	327	1968	4.00	3.25	2.10/2.45
283	1957–67	3.50	3.48	2.00/2.30	350	1967-	4.00	3.48	2.10/2.45
302	1967	4.00	3.00	2.00/2.30		Present			
302	1968–69	4.00	3.00	2.10/2.45	400	1970–80	4.125	3.750	2.10/2.65
305	1976-	3.767	3.480	2.10/2.45					

Source: Chevrolet Motor Div.

The potent LT1 powers the 1993 Z-28 and Trans Am. The 5.7 liter (350ci) small-block V-8 has some interesting new features: a reverse flow cooling system, a one-piece ram type intake manifold, redesigned exhaust manifolds, and a distributorless ignition system. Its output is 275hp. Chevrolet Motor Div.

Chapter 2

Rebuilding the 305/350

The unfortunate reality is that the motivating force of your Camaro or Firebird—the engine—will eventually expire. It is usually a gradual process. Blue smoke may start coming out of the tailpipes or the engine won't seem to make as much power as it used to. Or perhaps you've beaten on it too many times and something inside finally lets go. At this point you have to decide what to do with the car. If you conclude that

The 305/350ci small-block is a reliable, well-built engine that will last 100,000 miles and longer, provided it is well maintained and not abused. However, under hard usage, the possibility that something will break or wear out increases and there is no magical additive that will remedy the situation. Your only recourse is to rebuild the engine. While the engine is apart you can, for a modest cost, install stronger components but on the other hand, it is easy to go overboard and spend too much on parts that aren't necessary.

the engine is just tired, you may feel it's time to trade it in—a typical reaction. If you decide to hold on to the car, you'll want to have the engine rebuilt.

Once you decide to have the engine rebuilt, you open the door to myriad possibilities. You can have the engine rebuilt to exactly the same condition as when it left the factory, or more likely, you'll want to make improvements. These improvements can be a black hole when it comes to cost; one thing always leads to another, and then another. Just look at an engine rebuilding book and you'll realize that there are many operations and part substitutions that you can make. These may or may not be necessary on a

street engine. If you knew how engines are built at the factory you'd realize that they are, "slapped together" and yet, these engines can take an inordinate amount of abuse. What is even more amazing is the quality of some of the stock parts, and that they, too, can hold up.

Most American V-8 engines, including the small-block, are understressed when it comes to horsepower output. Compare the 240hp output of the 350 TPI to the 310hp from a 3.5 liter BMW engine. The

Some people don't bother changing the oil and filter. All that crud in the lifter valley—actually, it covers everything inside the engine—is the result of oxidized oil. When an engine is this neglected any new added oil quickly gets dirty. The only way to remove these deposits is to take the engine apart and have it cleaned. The sludge also holds heat generated by the engine and makes it run hotter. Changing the oil frequently is the answer.

The reason why this engine stopped running became obvious, once it was apart. It ran out of oil, causing the pistons to seize. Pistons in this condition make good paperweights.

One way to identify 1987 and later cylinder blocks is to look at the back to see if they are machined for a one-piece

rear seal. Such blocks use an aluminum retainer, as shown in the second photo.

BMW is putting out 1.47hp per cubic inch while the 350 is loafing along at 0.685hp per cubic inch. And the BMW engine is doing this reliably, as is the 350. There is room in the 305/350 for power modifications that can be made before you need to go into the engine. These encompass intake and exhaust system mods outlined in this book, and the result will be what is called a "mildly modified" street engine.

On the other hand, a "built" engine, can cost between $5,000 to $15,000. The reason is the cost of the parts themselves—how about $3,500 for a set of titanium connecting rods?—and the labor involved in having the engine blueprinted. Blueprinting means having the engine rebuilt to the specifications originally called for. For example, it is a rare occurrence when the intake ports of a cylinder head actually match specifications. At the same time, when the engine is assembled it has to be put together within

factory specifications. This requires hours and hours of checking and rechecking clearances.

Aren't all engines put together within factory specs? They are, but the factory specs allow for a certain amount of tolerance. For example, connecting-rod oil bearing clearance is 0.0008–0.0026in. You may have some bearings on the low side and some on the high side. That is considered acceptable on a street engine that isn't asked to produce a lot of power for a long period of time. Like everything else, however, there is an optimum clearance that will result in a stronger running engine. When an engine is blueprinted, all clearances are made as equal as possible to make sure that each cylinder produces exactly the same amount of power.

Here we'll look at basic engine rebuilding fundamentals and make suggestions that are worthwhile for the typical modified "street" engine. I emphasize the word street because some machining operations and parts may not be necessary for a street engine

A pre-1987 block that uses a two-piece rear seal.

Blocks that use factory hydraulic roller lifters (right) have their lifter bores machined flat. You can't use the factory type hydraulic roller lifters on earlier blocks.

The first step after disassembly is to have the block, heads, and other parts cleaned. Hot-tanking or running the parts through a jet cleaning booth is how this is accomplished, with the booth method taking a shorter time. If you aren't planning to work on the engine immediately, have all the parts sprayed with WD-40 to inhibit rust. The block should be dry Magnafluxed to see if any cracks are present. This is done by magnetizing the block and pouring a magnetic powder on the block. Some cracks or damaged areas can be repaired, thereby saving you the cost of a new block.

that will only on occasion see the high side of 6000rpm.

The typical enthusiast obviously cannot rebuild the engine completely by himself or herself because too many operations require the use of specialized equipment. For these, the parts will have to be sent out to the machine shop. However, many preparatory and assembly operations can be made with simple hand tools.

At best, this chapter is only an overview of the rebuilding process. For a more detailed look on engine rebuilding fundamentals you should get a copy of *How to Rebuild Your Small-Block Chevy* from HP Books, or *Engine Rebuild & Assembly Techniques* from Classic Motorbooks.

Tools

Car enthusiasts say that you can never have enough tools. This is true, but it can be surprising to know that you only need a few tools to take apart and put together an engine.

The first tool you'll need is a shop manual. Not only will critical specifications be listed, but the order in which things should be done will also be included. A general engine rebuilding book is good to have, but these won't tell you what you have to do to remove the engine from your Camaro's or Firebird's engine compartment. If you can, invest in a factory shop manual.

Basic hand tools are required, along with a good torque wrench. The click types are preferable because you can torque down bolts much faster. You'll also need a harmonic balancer puller and an engine

If the bores don't show much wear, you don't have to overbore the cylinders but most rebuilders will automatically overbore them 0.030in for quality control reasons. This is done in two steps: on the boring machine, shown here, and when the cylinders are honed. Because the cylinder block is a thin-wall design, you shouldn't overbore beyond 0.040in. Going to 0.060in over is common, but there is a small possibility that the resulting cylinder walls will be too thin.

Prior to align honing, the main cap bolts and threads should be clean in order to get a correct torque reading. Thread chasers and brushes are used here. With the main caps bolted in place, they are align honed on this machine. This ensures that the main bearing bores are perfectly round and in alignment with each other.

The final block machining operation is to have the cylinders honed. The type of finish depends on the type of piston ring used. It is extremely important to thoroughly clean the block after this operation to get rid of all the metal bits and grit that have accumulated. A machine shop will send the block through the jet booth but if you are doing this at home, start off with plenty of detergent and water. Use clean rags soaked in automatic transmission fluid to clean the cylinder bores.

stand in addition to a set of micrometers, a dial caliper, a dial indicator, a piston ring compressor, and a valve spring compressor tool. If you plan to do any porting, a die-grinder with a variety of stones and cutters will let you port your heads along with other operations such as engine block deburring and chamfering. You can also invest in other specialized tools, such as an inside micrometer, which can make a rebuild easier and quicker.

The Cylinder Block

Once you have removed the engine from the engine compartment, take that engine apart. Depending on the rebuild and your budget, it is unlikely that you'll reuse the pistons, camshaft, valve lifters, bearings, timing chain and gears, and oil pump. You'll probably reuse the pushrods, rockers, and maybe the valve springs and, unless there is a damaged rod, the connecting rods.

Once the engine is apart, you might as well take it to the rebuild shop that will perform the machining operations. They'll have the block and heads hot-tanked to get them degreased and cleaned. Some shops may use a jet cleaning booth, in which case long pipe brush cleaners will be used to make sure the oil passages are clean. All bolt holes should also be chased with an undersized tap to make sure they are clean.

After the block is clean, you'll be able to determine if the block can be reused. Every block should be Magnaflux inspected. In this process, magnetic powder is spread on a section of the block at a time while a large U-shaped magnet is moved over it. Any cracks will disrupt the magnetic field as the powder will collect on them, making cracks evident. Every surface of the block should be treated in this manner. You'll want to have additional tests performed, such

Next, new freeze plugs are installed. The sealer is used to ease installation.

Pay special attention to the rear camshaft plug. Be sure to put a layer of sealer on it. Any leak here after the engine is together and running will be a royal pain to fix.

After installing new camshaft bearings with the installation tool, liberally coat the new cam with lubricant and carefully slide it in. At this point, the block should be set on an engine stand. Although not absolutely necessary, a stand makes a rebuild a lot easier and quicker.

as a pressure test to determine if there are any water jacket leaks and sonic testing to check for cylinder wall thickness, if you are building a high-horsepower 305 or 350.

The majority of production engines used on the F-body small-block used a two-bolt main block. This is strong enough for a street engine but if you feel insecure, you can install nodular four-bolt caps, GM part number 3932482. Also available are steel billet

This is what happens when the engine is overrevved. The crank journals will have to be cut down if this crank is to be used again.

The crank should also be checked for cracks by having it Magnafluxed. Covering the crank with a special liquid will show up any tell-tale cracks under an ultraviolet light. Even the slightest hairline crack means that the crank is unusable.

The crank's journals are cut on a special machine. If the crank is going to sit around for a while before installation, *make sure you spray the journals with WD-40 to prevent rust formation.*

After cutting, the journals are polished and all the oil holes chamfered.

The finished crank, ready to be installed. All the oil passages have been chamfered in order not to cut the new bearing shells at installation. The tag on the crank indicates that it is for a 305ci engine, and that the main and rod journals have been ground 0.010in undersize.

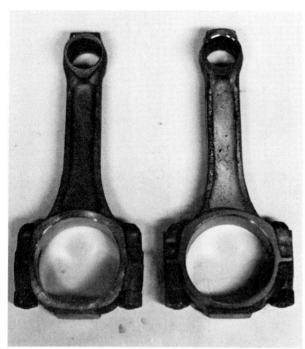

The stock 305/350 connecting rod (left) is strong enough for a street engine. For a high-performance application and some competition applications, you can use a "pink" rod, part number 14096846 (right). It is the same rod used on the LT1 and Z-28 engines and comes from the factory Magnafluxed and shot peened. It is designed for pressed-on wrist pins.

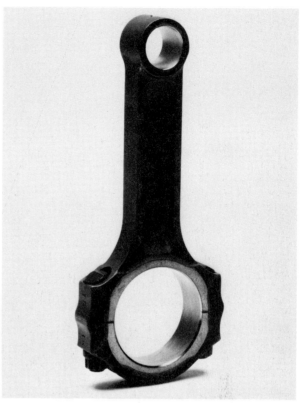

The ultimate in connecting rods are those made of titanium. They are super strong, super light, and as you can guess, super expensive. Crower Cams & Equipment Co.

Beyond the pink rod, there are many others to choose from. This is Crower's line of rods for use in the small-block.

There is one for every type of application and every budget. Crower Cams & Equipment Co.

Stock type pistons are made of cast-aluminum alloy and are dished because they have a low compression ratio. If you are installing a high-lift cam or perhaps intend to, this is the time to have the eyebrows enlarged. Pistons are always installed with the indentation toward the front of the block.

four-bolt caps that have a splayed bolt design—unnecessary but for all-out competition engines. If you have to replace the original block, you might as well use the heavy-duty 350ci bare block, part number 10105123 (10066098 for 305s). It is machined for hydraulic roller lifters and uses the newer one-piece rear main seals; however, you can use crankshafts that use the older two-piece main seal with adapter, part number 10051118. For a high-horsepower supercharged or a nitrous-equipped engine, there is the Bow Tie brand block, part number 10051183. This is a heavily reinforced block with siamesed cylinder walls.

The next step is to have the block deburred. All casting burrs, casting flash, and sharp edges are ground off because they can provide a starting point for cracks. Casting flash may also find its way to the oil pump and clog up the works. This may not be necessary in a street engine, but if you have the time it is a worthwhile operation.

The first major machining operation is align honing and boring. This operation ensures that the main bearing bores are aligned. The main bearing cap mating surfaces are ground to ensure they are flat and then reinstalled on the block. A boring or honing bar is then placed through the caps, with the end result of having main bearing bores that are round and in alignment with each other.

While align boring and honing should be considered necessary in every engine, having the block decked is another operation that is not absolutely

Install piston pins by heating the small end of the rod and then slipping in the pin. As the rod cools, a tight interference fit results.

With the rings installed, the piston-rod assemblies are lined up and ready to install in the cylinder block. To prevent any damage to the cylinders or crankshaft, these vinyl sleeves are placed over each rod bolt.

necessary in a street engine. Decking aligns the decks (the surface where the cylinder head is bolted) with each other and with the crankshaft. Sometimes you'll find that the decks aren't at quite a 90deg (degree) angle in relation to the crankshaft. Decking also establishes deck height, or the distance from the flat (quench) part of the piston to the deck surface on the block when the piston is at top dead center (TDC).

Most rebuilders will have the block deck surface milled slightly to ensure a good sealing surface for the head gaskets.

And most machine shops automatically replace the stock pistons with new 0.030in over pistons. To do this, the cylinders are overbored a corresponding amount in two operations—first on the boring machine which removes the bulk of material, and the balance when the cylinders are honed to the final, desired finish which is dependent on the type of piston rings to be used. Most 305/350s will end up with molybdenum rings which require little, if any, break-in. In this case, the cylinder walls will be finished with a fine 400 grit honing stone. Chrome-plated rings require a rougher finish. Chrome rings have a very hard surface and the rougher finish traps oil in the cylinder walls to provide lubrication for the rings. These rings are of little value in a street engine, however.

In some cases, engine builders use honing plates that are bolted on the deck surface to simulate the distortion caused by the cylinder head on the cylinder. Cylinders honed in this manner will be rounder and produce more power.

At this point, the block must be cleaned with detergent and water to remove the metal dust, chips, and grit on the block and especially the cylinder walls. It is also important to clean all the oil passages

The bare cylinder head should be Magnafluxed and visually checked for cracks after it comes out of the jet stream booth. If it passes, the cylinder head's surface is milled to provide a good sealing surface for the head gasket.

You can reuse the original valve springs, provided they are up to stock specifications. Here they are being checked on a special valve spring machine. If you are installing an aftermarket camshaft, you should install the springs that came with the cam kit.

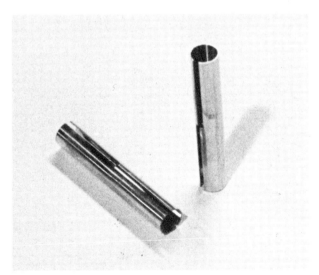

Bronze valve guides should always be installed. Their cost is modest and they will outlast any other reconditioning method.

The stock rocker arms and balls can also be reused, provided they aren't scored.

After the valve job has been performed, the valves are lapped. Lapping will show if the valve job has been done correctly or not and also ensures a good seal.

The main bearing shells are installed at this point—on the caps and on the block saddles. Make sure that they are lubricated before you place the crankshaft on them. If you are going to use the Plastigage method of measuring bearing clearance, this is the time to do it.

and to spray the entire block with a rust inhibitor. To make sure there is no abrasive grit on the cylinder walls, use paper towels soaked in automatic transmission fluid to scrub them clean. Use new towels until there are no more grit traces on the towels.

Crankshaft

All current F-body small-blocks come with a cast-iron crankshaft. Once again, you'll find this crank adequate for most street applications, but there is the forged steel crank available, part number 14096036. For pre-1986 engines, you can use part number 3941180 or 3941184 (nitride treated) which accept the two-piece rear main seal. The small-block is blessed with a very strong bottom end and crank breakage or oiling problems are not common.

Actually, there is not much that you can do with the crankshaft besides dropping it off at the crankshaft shop. There it will be checked for straightness and cracks. Even one slight crack will mean discarding the crank because cracks can't be repaired.

If needed, the journals will be cut undersize, and they should be micropolished and the oil holes chamfered. That's about all that is needed for a street engine.

Operations such as cross-drilling, tuftriding, and chroming aren't necessary on a street engine. If you are building a high-horsepower motor, then you should plan on getting either a semi-finished or unmachined forging from GM Performance Parts.

Factory crank bearing clearances are listed at 0.0008–0.0020in; 0.0008 is too tight for a performance

To avoid any possibility of mixing up the center three caps, lay them out prior to installation in the correct order. By this point, the cap bolts also should be cleaned and lightly oiled.

Install all the caps and torque them down to specifications. Then remove them to check bearing clearance. If there is too much or too little clearance, try switching the bearing shells or use another set.

Don't forget to check the crank thrust clearance with a dial indicator. After the caps are installed, spin the crank to make sure that its turns freely.

engine so you should aim for the high end of the tolerance limit. Very high-performance engines will typically have larger clearances, 0.0025–0.0035in. A looser fit will result in less friction but also requires an oiling system capable of supplying additional volume to the bearings. Bearing clearances should be checked; Plastigage is easy to use, if you don't have a micrometer. If the bearing clearance is too loose or too tight, you can use undersize or oversize bearings

The next step is to install the piston-rod assemblies. Turn the crank at bottom dead center (BDC) for each cylinder, as shown.

Using a ring compressor, lightly tap the piston in. Before you start, make sure that you oil each cylinder.

You can check rod side-to-side clearance with a feeler gauge. Hopefully, it will be within specs. If not you can switch the rods, have them refaced, or even replaced.

or even bearings made by a different manufacturer to arrive at the desired clearance.

In addition to bearing clearance, you also have to check for thrust clearance which measures the front-to-rear crankshaft motion.

Rods and Pistons

Stock 305/350 connecting rods are made from forged steel. This makes them reliable for street use but there are quite a number of factory and after-market alternatives available if you are building a high-horsepower engine. The least expensive way to go is to use the part number 14096846 "pink" (for its

Once the pistons are all in place, install the timing chain. Make sure the marks on the timing gears line up. This engine is using an iron gear which is preferable to the nylon type. With the timing chain installed, put on the timing cover, followed by the crankshaft balancer.

Bolt down the oil pressure relief valve housing. If you have a filer handy, hand tighten it now.

Next, bolt down the oil pump. Considering the cost of a new unit, use a new pump.

color code) rod. This is the same rod that came on the LT1, Z-28, and L82 1970s era small-blocks. Beyond this there are the Bow Tie rods, which are designed for competition use and use larger $^7/_{16}$in rod bolts.

As with the crankshaft, the connecting rods should first be checked for any twists or bends and then Magnafluxed for cracks. If they pass, the big end should be resized. This is done on a special machine. The process is similar to align honing the main caps. A small amount of metal is removed from the cap to make sure the mating surface is flat, and then reinstalled on the rod. The bore is then made perfectly round on the machine.

The oil pump pickup is a press-in fit to the pump. Use some antiseize compound to make sure that the pickup doesn't work itself loose. If it does, it will mean certain disaster.

Although not necessary on a street engine, you may want to have the side beams polished and shot peened. Like deburring the block, these steps eliminate the forging line and thus reduce the possibility for cracks to start. For added insurance, also replace the stock rod bolts with SPS type bolts.

As far as piston pin fit, there is no reason to switch from the stock pressed pin to a full-floating configuration. You know that the stock pressed-in pin is not going anywhere when there is a 0.0015in interference fit. Installation is accomplished by heating the rod small end and then the pin-piston assembly is slipped through. When the rod cools, the pin is locked in place.

Factory rod bearing clearance is listed as 0.0013–0.0035in; race engines will typically require more clearance, 0.0005–0.0010 beyond the upper end tolerance limit.

You can spend a lot of money on pistons but again, this is an area where you don't need to go too far beyond the stock cast pistons. Cast pistons are relatively inexpensive, they are lighter than most forged pistons, and they can be installed with less side clearance (because they don't expand as much as forgings) in the cylinder bore, thereby providing better ring seal which means more power. Forged pistons may work fine at high-rpm, high-heat situations but because they are installed with more side clearance, they are apt to be noisy and can increase oil consumption.

One noteworthy recent development in piston technology is the hypereutectic piston. These pistons are made from a special alloy and are cast at a higher temperature. The result is a strong, light piston that is almost as durable as a forging but without the forged piston's weak points. As you would expect, hypereutectic pistons cost more than regular castings but less than forged pistons. Hypereutectic pistons are installed in the 5.7 liter High Output engine and are

Install the oil pan gasket and then the oil pan itself.

Turn the block over, and put on the head gaskets.

available for other applications in a 9.8:1 compression ratio from GM Performance Parts.

Considering the octane of today's gasoline, it doesn't make much sense to go for a compression ratio that is more than 9.0:1 or so, unless you plan to use additives or you're building a race engine. Stick with the stock compression ratio.

One modification you may want to make before installing the pistons is to have valve reliefs cut a little deeper to compensate for any future higher lift cam installation, or if you are installing a higher lift cam now.

By far the most common piston rings used today are moly rings. They are made from cast iron that incorporates a molybdenum surface layer. Moly rings are long lasting, reliable, and require little break-in. One area that *could* use some improvement, though, is the oil control ring. The stock low-tension rings are supposed to increase horsepower but you're better off using TRW or Sealed Power rings which provide better oil control.

You can gain a few horses by using gapless piston rings. Total Seal Corporation of Phoenix, Arizona, produces a two-piece, double interlocking ring—each ring has a gap, but they occur at different positions so that there is no one gap for gases to escape. These rings will definitely add horsepower and at a very modest cost.

Cylinder Heads

Racers always put extra-special effort into cylinder head preparation—the cylinder heads, after all, are responsible for all that horsepower you're hoping your engine will make. As we will see in the intake chapter, chapter 3, the stock 305/350 heads are a fairly good design when it comes to valve size and porting but there are many ways to go if you're looking for something better. Besides following the usual reconditioning procedures, you can perform some basic porting on the stock heads to improve

flow, and remember, even the trick aftermarket heads will eventually need to be rebuilt.

The first step to take after removing the valves, rockers, and springs is to have the heads cleaned, either in the hot tank (not for aluminum heads!) or in the booth. At this point, visually inspect the heads for any cracks, especially around the exhaust seat area. Have the heads Magnafluxed as well.

Regardless of your intentions for your engine, even if going back to dead stock, you should have bronze valve guides installed. The valves in the cylinder head don't just go up and down; the rocker arms exert side-to-side pressures as well, which lead to guide wear. As the guides wear, the possibility for the valve not landing squarely on the seat also increases, allowing leaks to occur. Bronze valve guides last longer, require less lubrication than the stock iron guides, the valves can be fitted with less clearance, and the bronze guides transfer heat better from the valve to the head. The exhaust valves and seats are subjected to higher than ever temperatures,

The reconditioned heads are then put on the block.

Coat the lifters with oil and drop them in each lifter bore.

Slip in the pushrods, making sure that each end is coated with oil or moly type grease.

which contribute to valve seat erosion. The reason for this is that the fuel mixture during part-throttle operation is very lean—good for mileage, but it creates high combustion chamber temperatures. Exhaust valve and seat failure can also occur if there is a problem with your Camaro or Firebird's catalytic converters. If they get plugged up, the valve and seat temperature goes way up.

If you are on a very tight budget, the stock rockers can be refaced and reused if they aren't scored, but you are better off replacing them, especially if you are installing a new camshaft. You may reuse the stock valve springs provided they haven't lost any height and tension, but always use new valve keepers. Of course, if you are installing a new cam, it is always a good idea to replace the valve springs.

If you are going to reuse the stock valves, you'll gain significant airflow into and out of the engine if you have a three-angle valve job performed. The stock heads have seats ground at a single angle of 45 degrees—good for durability but not for optimizing flow. A three-angle valve job improves flow by smoothing out the flow of gases into and out of the combustion chamber.

It would also be a good idea to do any porting on the stock heads at this point. Refer to chapter 3,

which covers the induction system and cylinder heads.

Most rebuilders will mill the head a slight amount for better gasket sealing, usually in the area of 0.0005in. This may or may not be enough to warrant cutting the intake manifold or cylinder head manifold mounting surface to maintain port alignment.

Final Assembly and Break-in

Once all the parts have been reconditioned, all that is left is to put them back together. Make sure you have all the parts in one place and that you have all the nuts and bolts that you originally started out with. You can follow the rebuild procedures in the following photo essay which was performed on a stock 350 at Quality Engine Distributors in Middletown, New York.

When the engine is back in your car's engine compartment, run the engine at 1500–2000rpm for half an hour to break in the cam. Change the oil and filter immediately, check for any leaks, and then drive the car at moderate, varying speeds for about 500 miles. There are differing opinions on this as some will say that with moly rings, you don't need such a long break-in period, and this may be true for nine out of ten cars. Who wants to be the tenth car? Play it safe.

Initially, install the rockers loosely on each stud. Turn the engine so that the piston on cylinder one is at TDC. Tighten the rocker arm nut until you can feel the slack being taken up as you hold the pushrod. The pushrod should be easy to rotate. Then tighten the rocker arm nut $^1/_4$ turn more. Repeat the sequence until all cylinders are completed.

With the installation of the valve covers, the engine is painted and ready for the intake and exhaust manifolds and subsidiary systems such as the starter, distributor, water pump, and so forth, and back to your car's engine compartment. Don't forget to put in some oil!

Chapter 3

Induction System and Cylinder Heads

Your getting the most from your engine largely depends on how much air-fuel mixture you can get into it. The traditional way to improve the induction system has been to install a larger carburetor and a more efficient intake manifold. This seems fairly simple, but it has been a source of endless problems, not to mention magazine articles, over the years. One of the problems, or let's say characteristics of the induction system is that it is the most visible of any modifications that one can make. Consequently, there has been lots of romanticizing when it comes to the induction system—what looks good doesn't often run well on a street machine.

Carburetion

Carburetors were available on 305 (5.0 liter) engines during 1982–87. This was the familiar Rochester Quadrajet unit which was electronically controlled by the car's electronic control module (ECM) system.

In the past, Chevrolet performance engines came with aluminum high-rise intake manifolds— the best one originating in 1967 and used on the Z-28 engine. It was also used on the 1970-72 LT1 engine. Basically it consisted of refined dual-plane manifolds that followed stock configuration but had taller, larger passages for better engine breathing. Dual-plane types have also been known as the Cross-H or 180deg design, which was originated by Ford Motor Company in the early thirties. With this type, each half of the manifold feeds half the cylinders, and the two halves are not connected. It is called a 180-degree

Typical 1980s style low-power small-blocks came with a Rochester Quadrajet or a throttle body injection (TBI) system. They are typified by a restrictive intake manifold and an equally restrictive air cleaner. The only positive aspect of the stock system is the use of a fresh-air intake for the air cleaner. Simply replacing these components with a tried and true performance intake and carburetor will result in a substantial increase in power—provided you also make the necessary modifications to the exhaust system.

The stock Quadrajet carburetor is known as a spread-bore design because it uses two very small primaries with two larger secondaries. The advantages of a spread-bore are very good low-speed throttle response and economy. A disadvantage is the great air-fuel mixture velocity difference between the two sets of throttle bores that occurs when the large secondaries open up.

design because the engine draws alternately from each manifold half as it moves through the firing cycle. The dual-plane manifold provides excellent throttle response and low- to mid-range power. However, it tends to become restrictive at high rpm.

The familiar Holley four-barrel has its four throttle bores more equally spaced. Certain high-performance manifolds have a base that is drilled to accept both carburetor types.

These three intake manifolds for the small-block Chevy are from Edelbrock Corp. The Performer is a good choice for a basically stock engine and is designed to increase power in the 1000–5000rpm range. For a more modified engine, the Performer RPM moves its operational range up 500rpm to 1500–5500. Both the Performer and Performer RPM are of the traditional dual-plane design. The Performer is designed to accept both spread-bore and Holley pattern carburetors. The Torker II is a single-plane design that continues making power to 6500rpm. Edelbrock Corp.

The other single four-barrel or X-type design that has been used successfully is the single-plane manifold. Here, all the manifold runners are connected to a common chamber or plenum and are fed by a single carburetor. It is a simple design, but single-plane manifolds really came into their own when Edelbrock refined the design in the late 1960s to provide superior performance over the dual-plane design. These manifolds have been developed and refined to such an extent that they match the low- and mid-range response of the dual-plane manifolds while surpassing them at higher rpm. Most, if not all, of the newer single-plane manifolds look very much alike. Usually, it is best to follow the manufacturer's recommendations according to your intended usage.

At this point you have to decide the route you're going to follow. Are you planning to remain totally legal, or modify your present system for off-road use? To remain legal, you have to retain the existing carburetor or replace it with another certified legal unit. Besides the stock carburetor, Holley has a 650cfm vacuum secondary spread-bore for 1982–83 305s that retains all factory computer controls. It is available under GM part number 0-80073. You should see some improvement over the stock Quadrajet. Besides this, though, your only other option is to remove the stock carburetor and manifold and replace them with aftermarket units. The cost is reasonable, $500 or less for a new carburetor and manifold. However, you'll have to disable the ECM unit and replace the stock distributor with an older unit that has mechanical and vacuum advance. Your local salvage yard should help in this area.

In terms of carburetors, there are several ways to go. The well-known Holley carburetors are available in many configurations, or you can have the stock Rochester modified, or you can use a Carter AFB which is now available through Edelbrock. You'll find proponents and strong-running engines with each type. Holley carburetors have been synonymous with performance for decades and you can't go wrong in choosing the brand. They are easy to modify because of their modular design, and are available in a spread-bore design, which is similar to the stock Quadrajet because they use two small primary bores and two much larger secondary bores. The reasons for the small primaries are better driveability at low speeds and better mileage. The more common Holley four-barrel pattern uses four throttle bores that are more equal in size, a preferable characteristic for a high-performance application.

A point worth considering with carburetors is whether to retain vacuum secondary operation or switch to a mechanical secondary carburetor, a category that includes Holley's double-pumpers. The secondary two-barrels on a vacuum secondary controlled carburetor open up upon engine demand, therefore it is difficult to overcarburet with such a unit. With mechanical secondaries, an oversize carburetor will result in bogging (hesitation) when the throttle is floored, not to mention poor fuel economy.

If you decide to replace the stock carburetor with a Holley, in my opinion, there is nothing better than one of Holley's double-pumpers. I've found that they idle better and create more power. These carburetors have a mechanical secondary operation and use two accelerator pumps. For optimum results, however, additional modifications should be contemplated, such as a stouter camshaft, freer-flowing cylinder heads, and exhaust system mods. Holley part number 0-4776 flows 600cfm, 0-4777 is at 650cfm, and so on to 850cfm. Which is best for your 305? Again, it depends on what other modifications you have made. A slightly modified engine will work well with a 600 or 650cfm unit while a more modified engine may tolerate a larger carburetor. More often, though (especially in magazines), you'll find that the 750cfm vacuum secondary Holley, part number 0-3310, is recommended.

One of the major complaints that you'll hear if you decide to go the carburetor route is that a carburetor is basically a crude device that lacks the inherent adjustability of electronic fuel injection to adapt to changing conditions. This is true, particularly from an emissions output standpoint, but you can go a long way toward eliminating some of these drawbacks with Holley's Quarter-Mile-Dial electronic fuel bowl system. Through the use of a dash-mounted control you can electronically change the fuel mixture from $1/3$ to 10 jet sizes. This is a real time saver and you are even able to adjust the air-fuel ratio between the primary and secondary side of the carburetor to compensate for any intake manifold distribution peculiarities. The bowls can be retrofitted on existing carburetors or you can get them on brand-new carburetors.

With most aftermarket carburetors you'll find that your engine will not ping if you disconnect your EGR (exhaust gas recirculation) valve. That is because they are calibrated for maximum power—meaning that they may be on the rich side.

But maximum power output is not the primary aim of the stock carburetor (or fuel injection, for that matter). Its primary goal is to meet federal emission standards. Once that has been accomplished, driveability, ease of starting, maximum power, and other considerations come into play. In an ideal situation, there would be an air-fuel ratio of 14.7:1 if all the fuel in the combustion chamber would be perfectly mixed and burned. This rarely happens, however. For an engine to make maximum power, all the air that went into the combustion chamber has to be used up, and to ensure that this happens, an excess of fuel has to be introduced. Sometimes additional fuel is also introduced to cool the engine. Naturally, this does not make for a clean, nonpolluting engine.

The opposite occurs for a carburetor calibrated for maximum fuel economy. In this situation, to get the most out of the fuel that is in the combustion chamber, an excess of air has to be introduced, resulting in air-fuel mixtures as high as 18:1. The excess air ensures complete fuel combustion.

Since the early 1970s, EGR valves have been used to recirculate a portion of the spent and partially spent exhaust gases into the combustion chamber to reduce emissions, usually to the tune of 10 percent. The valve opens only at part-throttle openings, such

Another good choice for a street engine is Holley's Street Dominator dual-plane intake. Note how the exhaust crossover passage runs underneath the carburetor plenum. The passages on the cylinder heads should not be blocked off on a street engine because they aid in quick warmup. On a competition engine, they can be blocked off. A cooler, denser fuel mixture makes more power. Holley Replacement Parts Div.

Don't know what carburetor or camshaft to install? Edelbrock has grouped its Performer RPM with the Edelbrock AFB carburetor and a compatible camshaft in a kit. They are all designed to work together for maximum output. Edelbrock Corp.

as when the vehicle is cruising. Obviously an engine doesn't run on spent gases, but these gases enable the engineer to lean out the carburetor further for better fuel economy because they help to cool the hot combustion chamber. Lean fuel mixtures increase combustion chamber temperatures dramatically. Thus the use of the EGR valve on a basically stock engine can be beneficial, but if you are looking for maximizing power output and have made the appropriate changes in your induction system, an EGR valve is unnecessary.

Like all the other parts of your engine, the manifold and carburetor you choose will work best when they are compatible with the rest of your engine—specifically the camshaft, exhaust system, and rear axle gears. There is no point in overfilling the cylinders if you can't get the spent gases out quickly enough.

Recommendations

As for specific intake manifold recommendations, on carbureted engines you can't go wrong by using the updated version of the Z-28/LT1 intake manifold. Available from GM under part number 10185063, it is the same unit that comes on the 350 HO engine. This latest version has a dual mounting flange to accommodate a Quadrajet or a Holley type four-barrel carburetor. It also has all the necessary fittings and bosses for all late-model air conditioning brackets and emissions fittings—and it is designed to clear the Camaro and Firebird hood.

Beyond what you can get from Chevrolet, there is Edelbrock's Performer RPM and the Torker, both of which require a more modified engine in order to realize their full potential. Holley also offers their dual-plane Contender four-barrel manifold which is similar to the Chevrolet Z-28 piece. These manifolds can be made to work on the street, as can other more exotic intake types such as two four-barrel or three two-barrel multiple carburetor manifolds. It is not just a matter of bolting them on, however, but carefully selecting and matching the rest of your engine's components so they all work together to maximize output while retaining as much driveability as possible. To fully take advantage of a manifold that breathes better at higher rpm requires that at the very least, the camshaft and cylinder heads allow for the extra flow.

In terms of carburetion, depending on your brand preference, for a high-performance street engine pick a carburetor in the 600–700cfm range and you'll be in the ball park. A more modified engine can use more intake mixture, but here it is best to follow the intake manifold manufacturer's recommendations.

Electronic Fuel Injection

The use of a four-barrel carburetor represented 1960s technology adapted to the harsh (emissions-

To get the most out of a new intake-carburetor system you'll either have to modify the stock ECM to work together with the new components, or disable the system and install an older mechanical/vacuum advance distributor as has been done here.

Carbureted (and TBI) 305s will benefit from the use of a large, unrestrictive air cleaner assembly. The stock air cleaner, even with the two inlets on the L69 HO engine, limits airflow, making the carburetor flow less than its 600cfm capacity. The only drawback with this particular setup is that the engine doesn't benefit from ingesting cooler, denser outside air. This air cleaner is from Moroso Performance Products, Inc.

wise) reality of the 1980s, but it was at best a stopgap measure. Getting more power from the small-block and still meeting emission regulations while maintaining the driveability and fuel economy that a street car requires meant the use of a fuel injection system.

A fuel injection system is inherently more efficient than carburetion, but it is also more complex. In a carburetor, as air is pulled through the component, fuel is also pulled and mixed into this air stream, which is then distributed to each cylinder via the intake manifold. In a fuel injection system, rather than the fuel passively mixing in the air stream, fuel injectors squirt a predetermined amount of fuel into the air stream just as the intake valve begins to open. Fuel injection systems can be mechanically or electronically controlled; all current fuel injected engines use electronically controlled systems.

All current electronic fuel injection systems can be divided into three types by the method used to measure the airflow that the engine is using. Based on this airflow measurement, an electronic computer (in this case, the ECM) calculates the amount of fuel that has to be injected into each cylinder and then sends an appropriate electronic signal to the injector, allowing it to open.

The first system, used on throttle body fuel injection, is relatively simple—it uses throttle position and engine rpm as the basis for airflow calculations.

The top engine option on 1982–83 F-bodies was the dual throttle body injected 305. The system was known as the Cross-fire Injection System (CIS). It used two throttle bodies mounted on opposite sides of the intake manifold, with the right unit feeding the

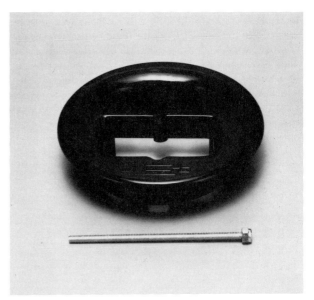

Using an induction stack can increase airflow through your carburetor, provided you have at least 2in clearance between the stack and the air cleaner top. This one is designed to be used with a Holley carburetor. Mr. Gasket Co.

Another inexpensive way to get the most from your carburetor is to use an insulating spacer. It reduces heat flow to the carburetor and the additional height adds velocity at high rpm. Mr. Gasket Co.

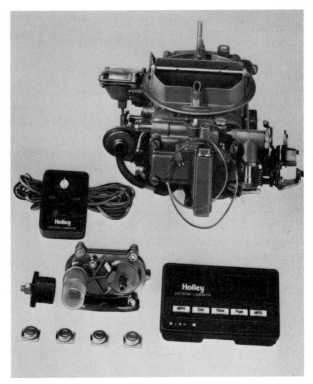

One of the main complaints against using carburetors is that they lack the precision of an electronic fuel injection system. That may be true, but they also lack the very high cost of an EFI system. With Holley's Electronic Carburetor System you can adjust the air-fuel ratio from the dash, maximizing power and economy. You can install a complete electronic carburetor or just a kit to upgrade an existing carburetor. Holley Replacement Parts Div.

left side and the left unit the right side. A lot of hoopla was made about the system, but the throttle body's flow capacity was small, and late in the 1983 model year the system was replaced by a conventional Rochester Quadrajet four-barrel carburetor which was simpler and also produced 25hp more.

From 1988 on, all base 305s got a throttle body fuel injection system that is regulated and controlled by the ECM computer. The throttle body resembles a

Holley carries these Pro-Jection TBI conversion kits for carbureted engines with either two or four injectors. The kits use a Holley bolt pattern and come complete with a control unit and fuel pump. The two-barrel version flows 670cfm which is enough for an engine producing up to 320hp while the larger unit flows 900cfm—good for up to 600hp. Holley also has systems that flow 2,200cfm for racing use. Holley Replacement Parts Div.

two-barrel carburetor, sharing the same bolt pattern, and it also uses the same intake manifold. Two downward-pointing fuel injectors are housed in the throttle body which spray fuel into the throttle body valves and the intake manifold. An electric fuel pump, located in the fuel tank, supplies the throttle body with fuel where a fuel pressure regulator maintains a pressure of 9–12psi (pounds per square inch). Compared to other systems, throttle body systems have very few sensors and are more user adjustable.

There is not much that you can do to increase the performance of a 305 throttle body injection system. It is possible to substitute a throttle body from a larger Chevrolet engine but there again, the restrictive nature of the intake manifold will limit power.

To improve power on a throttle body system, you should use an aftermarket intake manifold, such as Edelbrock's Performer with a two-to-four barrel carburetor adapter for the throttle body. All the benefits of the improved manifold should be evident with throttle body injection.

In 1985 the Rochester four-barrel carburetor was replaced by a multipoint, pulse time, mass airflow fuel injection system. Incorporated in the TPIS (Tuned Port Intake System) is the second system for measuring airflow, the air meter types, of which the Mass Air Flow system is one. All 1985–89 engines were equipped with Bosch Mass Air Flow units. The only difference from a Speed Density system, the third system, as used in 1990–93 engines, is that a Mass Air Flow system measures all the airflow that goes into the engine through an airflow sensor built into the air intake system. Through the use of the Mass Air Flow

Chevrolet's 1982–83 Crossfire Injection System used two throttle bodies. Small cubic-foot-per-minute capacity restricted output, though, and it was replaced by carburetors on later engines.

The Tuned Port Injection system was first used in 1987 on 305 and 350ci engines. A fairly sophisticated system, it delivers excellent fuel economy, low-end torque, and throttle response up to about 4500rpm. Small internal passages limit horsepower above this point. There are certain things the enthusiast can do to improve the stock system but for a significant increase in power, comparable to an aftermarket intake manifold and carburetor, the system needs to be replaced.

(MAF) sensor and various other sensors, the density and fuel requirements of the engine are calculated by the ECM processor. All the information gathered from these sensors is compared to a preprogrammed table stored in the computer. That table's data is based on the volumetric efficiency of a stock engine. As long as the computer "sees" sensor readings that are recognizable, the engine runs fine.

The Mass Air Flow sensor used on the TPI (Tuned Port Injection) engines is a Bosch unit that uses a heated platinum wire to measure airflow. This wire is heated to about 100 degrees higher than the incoming air. As the incoming air rushes over the wire, it cools the wire. To maintain the same temperature, additional voltage is fed to the wire. Based on these voltage fluctuations, a signal is sent to the ECM and from this, the correct fuel mixture and ignition curve are calculated. The MAF measures four attributes of the incoming air which allows for more precise fuel delivery. They are volume, air temperature, barometric pressure, and humidity.

Volume: As more air flows through the sensor, such as occurs under acceleration, the incoming air will cool the wire. As more voltage is fed to the wire to maintain temperature, the ECM accordingly increases fuel flow to the injectors.

Air Temperature: Colder air will cool the wire but also consider that colder air is more dense. The additional voltage sent to the wire will signal the ECM to increase fuel flow and vice versa.

Barometric Pressure: As weather (and altitude) changes, barometric pressure changes as well. Lower barometric pressure causes the intake air to be less

dense which means that it will have less of a cooling effect on the wire and vice versa. Once again, the ECM will respond to compensate for any barometric changes to maintain correct fuel flow.

Humidity: Humidity decreases air density, so the ECM compensates for any humidity changes.

The MAF measures all these characteristics simultaneously—allowing for very accurate airflow measurements, which translates to better engine

For modified TPI engines, SLP Engineering offers this modified throttle body which has a 17 percent larger opening area. They recommend using it only on engines that are modified to produce 350hp and more, such as cars that run in the high 12sec range in the quarter with slicks. Otherwise, you won't see any increase. SLP Engineering, Inc.

TPI Specialties also has a variety of throttle bodies available, all designed to flow more than the stock unit (top). The stock unit has TPI Specialties' airfoil installed which increases flow from the stock 668 to 709cfm. TPI Specialties, Inc.

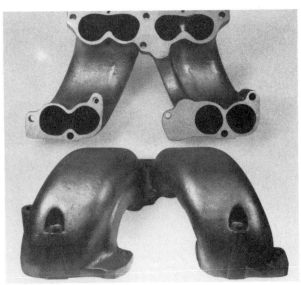

A popular modification to the stock TPI is to replace the stock intake runners. These runners connect the plenum to the intake manifold base. There are several ways to go here. SLP recommends siamesed runners over larger individual tube runners. SLP Engineering, Inc.

performance. The MAF also has a self-cleaning feature. After the engine is shut off, the wire will be heated red-hot for about one second, to burn off any dirt that may have covered the wire which would cause inaccurate readings.

In the Speed Density system, a Manifold Absolute Pressure (MAP) sensor measures the changes in intake manifold and from this, the ECM calculates the correct fuel and ignition requirements for the engine. A Speed Density system is therefore accurate for only a particular set of variables. If, for example, you increase airflow into the engine, the ECM won't know it. All it will know, based on information from the MAP sensor, is to increase fuel based on the stock airflow measurements built into the ECM. Even though the engine is now getting more air, the ECM can't compensate by increasing fuel delivery, so the engine runs lean.

Thus the primary advantage of a Mass Air Flow over a Speed Density system for the street is that the Mass Air Flow system allows for additional engine modifications without the usual driveability problems associated with a modified engine using the latter system. A better understanding of how both systems work can be had once open loop and closed loop computer operations are explained.

Open Loop and Closed Loop

The electronic control module computer operates in two modes—open and closed loop. The engine operates in the open loop mode primarily when the engine is started. This translates into a spark curve that is slightly more advanced and a richer fuel mixture to keep the engine running. The engine also runs in open loop mode when certain sensors have failed. As the coolant temperature approaches 150 degrees Fahrenheit, the computer gradually backs off on the timing and mixture.

In the closed loop mode, the computer analyzes all incoming data to achieve a chemically correct or stoichiometric fuel mixture which has an air-fuel ratio of 14.7:1. As mentioned earlier, this is the ideal situation where all the fuel is, in theory, perfectly mixed and ignited in the combustion chamber.

The primary sensor used in both open and closed loop modes is the oxygen sensor located in the exhaust system. The oxygen sensor measures the amount of oxygen that is in the exhaust. Because it is a transducer, the oxygen sensor converts the amount of oxygen content into an electrical impulse—which the computer is programmed to recognize. For example, if oxygen sensor output is 0.1 to 0.33 volt, then the engine is running too lean as oxygen is present in the exhaust. Conversely, if the reading is 0.8 to 1.1 volts, then the engine is running too rich as no oxygen is found in the exhaust.

The sensor that takes precedence over all others as far as the computer is concerned is the oxygen

Regardless what you do to the stock runners and plenum, there is only so much air that can flow through the stock manifold base, even if it has been ported. To get more air into the engine you need a better flowing system. TPI Specialties has their Big Mouth base which flows enough air for over a 1hp per cubic inch output. TPI Specialties, Inc.

The difference between the stock intake base and TPI Specialties' Big Mouth base is shown here. Bigger pas-

sages and openings translate into more airflow and therefore increased power. TPI Specialties, Inc.

sensor. The readings that it takes are the ones on which the computer is programmed to base all its subsequent decisions. Thus it doesn't pay to try and fool the computer by disabling certain sensors since the oxygen sensor will note any changes in the exhaust and instruct the computer to compensate, that is, to bring the system back to acceptable emission levels.

The ability to compensate is built into the system—not to thwart the hot rodder, but to enable the system to adjust for aging sensors and any manufacturing tolerances of the entire system. The computer has a correction table in its memory for each sensor and it automatically adjusts the system according to these factors.

Problems occur when the computer doesn't recognize the incoming data from the oxygen sensor —such as in a Speed Density system that has a non-stock camshaft. The computer tries to match the incoming information with the data in its memory, something that can't be done because it isn't there. As the computer searches for the correct setting, the engine will idle erratically and incorrect timing and fuel mixture conditions can occur as well. As long as the engine is stock, the closed loop mode works perfectly well with the Speed Density system.

By adding information from the airflow sensor in a Mass Air Flow system, the computer can compensate for any anomalies encountered in a mildly modified engine. Thus idle quality and driveability are once again possible in a dual-purpose car.

In both Speed Density and Mass Air Flow systems, however, at wide-open throttle (WOT) the ECM computer is programmed to maximize power, irrespective of any parameters relating to emission quality. Thus the EGR valve is closed, ignition timing is maximized, and the fuel curve is calibrated for maximum power.

Mass Air vs. Speed Density Systems

As stated earlier, 1985–89 TPI small-blocks came with a Mass Air Flow system and 1990–93 engines use a Speed Density system. If you have a 1990–93 engine and want to convert to a MAF system you'll have to install a MAF sensor along with a new harness (TPI Specialties, Incorporated has them) and a new Programmable Read Only Memory, or PROM, for your ECM. Once you do so, you have the ability to make further changes to your system without negatively affecting driveability.

Fuel Injection Modifications

Intake Tract

Before rushing out to spend a lot of money on the quest for better induction, you should first maximize the potential from what you already have.

Edelbrock's High-Flo manifold base—another good design. For best results, use Edelbrock's High-Flo runners. Edelbrock Corp.

To go beyond the capabilities of a stock or modified stock type system, you'll have to go for a system that has been designed for performance. One such system is the TPI Specialties Mini-Ram manifold. Like most performance setups, you'll give up a little on the bottom end but more than make up for it beyond 3500rpm. TPI Specialties, Inc.

You can achieve a noticeable improvement in output by removing obstructions in the stock air tract.

The Firebird and Camaro use different air intake systems, with the Firebird system being less efficient. The Camaro picks up air from the front of the engine via a plastic intake tract mounted on top of the

SLP's T-Ram manifold is used on the Firehawk and is designed to produce 50hp and 50lb-ft torque more than the stock system. It also looks pretty trick. SLP Engineering, Inc.

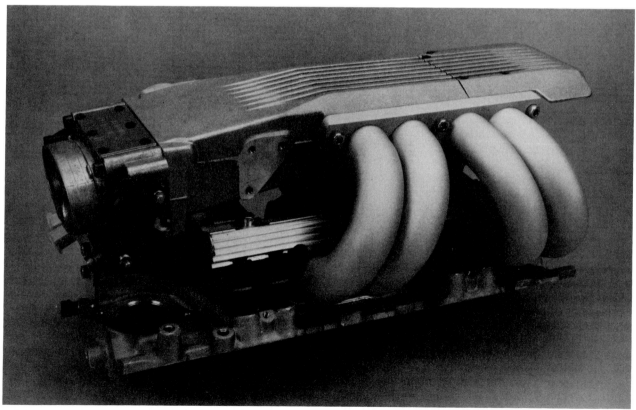

A highly regarded system, available from Arizona Speed & Marine. Resembling the stock system, it is actually extensively modified and an excellent choice for a street F-body. Arizona Speed & Marine

radiator. The Firebird gets its air from the left front area.

To get more out of the stock Firebird system, you can modify the stock air cannister by cutting its sides out. This will result in a 47cfm increase over the stock 1988 Trans Am air filter can. You should also substitute the stock air filter element with a less restrictive aftermarket unit such as one available from TPI Specialties or Hypertech which results in a small cubic-foot-per-minute gain and also provides superior filtration.

Better yet, install a complete Tuned Port Injection cold air induction system available from General Motors and SLP Engineering, Incorporated. It consists of a low-restriction air box that picks up air from the existing opening on the right-side inner fender.

The box is connected to the MAF via a ribbed duct which contains a directional vane designed to eliminate turbulence. Another duct connects the MAF to the throttle body. The system increases flow by 20 percent over the factory 1988–89 system and even more on the 1985–87 cars which had even more restrictive systems. Simply installing this kit will result in a 12–15hp increase.

When installing this kit in a Camaro, the battery must be relocated to the driver's side, in the same location as in the Firebird. The kit does include a new battery cable and necessary connectors.

The next area where you can reduce restriction is in the MAF sensor. According to TPI Specialties, a stock MAF sensor will flow 529cfm. If you remove the sensor from your car, you'll notice that there are screens at each end of the unit to protect the

The Lingenfelter box intake can be used with the stock runners and manifold base or with the Lingenfelter base and runners. The box layout is designed to increase low-end torque while maintaining high-rpm flow.

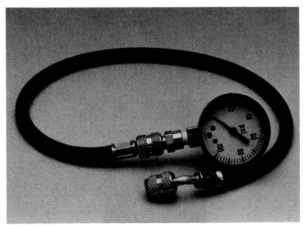

To accurately determine what pressure your stock fuel regulator puts out or what an aftermarket adjustable unit does, you'll need a fuel pressure test gauge. It connects to the fuel rail via a Schraeder valve. TPI Specialties, Inc.

Camaros (first photo) have used this type of air intake tract. While more efficient than the system used on

Firebirds (second photo) you'll see an improvement if you use a more efficient system.

platinum wire from any debris that might get through the air filter. The screens are held in place by a glued-on plastic ring. By removing the screens, you increase the flow through the MAF from 529 to 711cfm. An additional 39cfm can be obtained by hacksawing the seven aluminum heat sinks out for a total flow of 750cfm. Removing the heat sinks changes the unit's calibration which results in a leaned-out condition at 4250rpm and above. According to tests performed by TPI Specialties, a modified MAF sensor will result in a 5–10hp increase up to 4250rpm, but the leaned-out condition will reduce power from stock. This can be averted through the use of an adjustable fuel regulator and a redefined PROM—something you'd want to do anyway since they are necessary if you are looking for more than minor power increases.

As long as you are removing restrictions through the intake air tract, you can install a TPI Specialties throttle body airfoil. A stock throttle body will flow 668cfm, but with the airfoil, flow increases to 709cfm. On a modified engine, the airfoil is worth about 5–12hp.

A point worth remembering is that all this is dry airflow. In a carburetor, it is wet airflow because fuel is mixed in. Thus a 668cfm stock throttle body has the same capacity as a 750cfm carburetor, which is more than enough for an engine producing over 400hp.

The throttle body itself on the stock system uses two throttle valves and it is the least restrictive part encountered thus far. A larger throttle body is not necessary on a hot street engine, unless the engine has the capacity to use the extra airflow afforded by a larger throttle body. For a high-performance street engine, the emphasis so far has been to smooth out and reduce intake restrictions. In fact, it has been the equivalent of installing a large, free-flowing air cleaner assembly on a carbureted engine.

Fuel System

You wouldn't think so, but increasing fuel pressure to the injectors will result in more power. The reason is that more pressure produces a better injector spray pattern which results in better fuel atomization. Better atomization means the fuel is more completely burned so the oxygen sensor sees a slightly leaner situation and therefore adjusts the injector pulse width for more fuel, resulting in more power. Tests have borne this out and if you'll look at GM's recommended fuel pressure chart, fuel pressure

Fuel injected engines can benefit just as much from a ram air system as carbureted engines can. However, the true benefits are not from the negligible ram air effect but from feeding the engine cooler, denser air. This is a kit from SLP which draws cooler, denser air from an opening on the right front inner fender. When installed in a Camaro, the battery has to be relocated to the driver's side. SLP Engineering, Inc.

This is an improvement over the stock air box; however, the filter can still pick up hotter underhood air.

A good quality air filter is a must—it provides sufficient air flow without the least amount of restriction while filtering the air. These filters from Hypertech provide high quality and low restriction. Hypertech

has increased over the years on what is basically the same system. Also, not all engines are equipped with a high-pressure regulator and some may not even be set at the correct pressure. TPI Specialties and Hypertech both offer adjustable regulators.

The other area in the fuel system that needs some attention is the fuel injectors themselves. The Chevrolet small-block uses Bosch fuel injectors which are calibrated to flow at different rates depending on the engine (see chart). However, you'll find in a typical engine that not all injectors flow at the same rate. TPI Specialties has done extensive testing here as well and has found that there can be a 20 percent difference in flow rates among the eight injectors used in an engine. This is a considerable difference and helps to account for the fact that some cars equipped with identical engines are slower than others. The stock 305 injector is designed to flow 74 to 76ml (milliliter), but TPI Specialties has found that stock injectors can vary from 64 to 82. The 350 injectors should flow 85 to 88ml but they range from 80 to 95. Given the variance of stock injectors, an equalized set will result in more power—or let's say, you'll get the power you're supposed to be getting from a stock engine. Obviously, you should use a set of injectors that have been blueprinted, a service TPI Specialties provides.

The other point concerns injector flow rates. The 305 injector flows at 17lb/hr while the 350 injector flows at 22lb/hr. This is sufficient for a 305 producing more than 350hp and a 350 producing over 450hp. TPI Specialties tests have shown that for stroked small-blocks—383, 406, or 415ci—the hot setup is using a 305 injector with pressure set at 50psi. This combination makes more power than using 350ci injectors. So the bottom line seems to be that it isn't necessary to change from the stock fuel injectors for the bulk of high-performance applications. Just make sure they all flow the same rate and run a higher than stock pressure.

Fuel Injection Manifolds

Most factory carburetor manifolds have been designed for low-rpm response and driveability with

The stock Chevy cylinder head. Although there have been variations over the years, the basic design is the same as it was in 1955. Its strengths include the use of adjustable rockers, reasonable weight, and very good port configuration, especially on the exhaust side. The stock head, with minor modifications, is adequate for a high-performance street car. For an engine that is designed to rev over 6000rpm regularly, you may want to consider a cylinder head that flows more air.

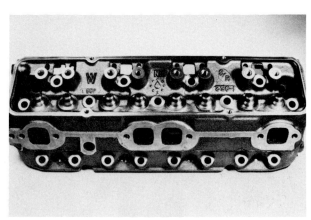

A well-known name in replacement cylinder heads is Dart. This particular head is the Dart S/R (Street Replacement) head for the small-block. It comes with either 67 or 76cc combustion chambers and the intake runner capacity is 171cc. You'll often see among cylinder head specifications figures given for intake runner capacity. One of the weak points of the small-block cylinder head is the intake port. Various aftermarket and Chevrolet heads come with larger capacity intake ports which make for higher flow. Such cylinder heads aren't advisable on the street, however, because a very high lift cam and high engine speeds are needed to take advantage of them. World Products, Inc.

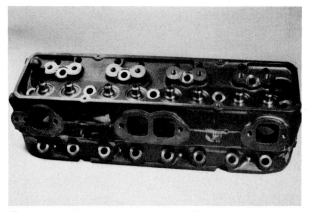

For competition use or very large displacement engines, there is the Dart II Sportsman head. It can accommodate valves measuring 2.08x1.625in intake/exhaust and has a larger 200cc intake runner. It is also available in aluminum. World Products, Inc.

little or no potential beyond 4500rpm. The manifold used on the Tuned Port Injection system is no different in this respect and it is an impediment to further horsepower gains. Still, there are things you can do to improve flow on the stock manifold.

The stock manifold is comprised of three sections—the bottom base, the runners, and the plenum on which the throttle body is mounted. The plenum and the base are connected by the tubular runners. You can remove the protruding castings that impede airflow at the plenum entry and also increase the size of the ports onto which the runners are bolted. There are aftermarket runners available from several sources which are designed to increase flow and power. SLP offers cast-aluminum siamesed runners while TPIS offers siamesed runners as well as larger

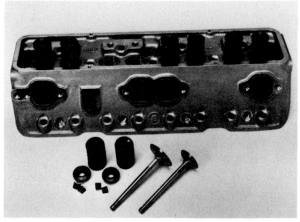

Another cylinder head that delivers is the street Brodix head. It comes complete with valves and springs, or bare. Brodix, Inc.

than stock diameter tube runners. No matter how good these runners are, though, the limiting factor is the restrictive stock manifold base. Besides having a poor entry angle, the runner volume in the manifold is not high enough to allow for free breathing. The only thing you can do is to replace the unit.

TPI Specialties has its Big Mouth intake manifold which flows enough air to allow for over 1hp per cubic inch output. On a dead-stock engine, the manifold itself is worth 22hp. Lingenfelter Performance Engineering also has a modified stock-type base.

The 1993 LT1 differs from the previous TPI engines in that it uses a one-piece intake manifold. Its shorter runners make more horsepower and provide a flatter and wider torque curve—at the expense of 15lb-ft of torque. However, the manifold, in stock form, has the potential to make a lot more horsepower on a modified engine. It is also almost identical to the TPI Specialties Mini Ram intake.

Beyond this, there are complete intake setups available from several sources that use either the stock, a modified stock base, or a new base section along with trick runners and plenums. The Arizona Speed & Marine TPI system resembles the factory system but uses a 58mm (millimeter) throttle body and a modified stock base. It is a good street type unit that maximizes output along factory parameters. Going beyond a modified stock system, the highly regarded TPI Specialties Mini Ram system resembles the 1993 LT1 system and will continue producing power at higher rpms as well. SLP's Short Ram Intake manifold resembles the traditional tunnel ram manifold and is designed to flow the amount of air needed for a high-revving modified engine. Lingenfelter of-

This is what the late-model stock small-block combustion chamber looks like. With a valve size of 1.94x1.50in intake/ exhaust, it can form the basis for a very strong running street car. Changing to high-performance cylinder heads should only be contemplated after you've taken steps to clean up the stock intake and exhaust system.

A stock Corvette aluminum head that has received some minor massaging. The valves have been unshrouded and the casting ridge beneath the valve seat has been smoothed out as well. These minor changes along with matching the intake and exhaust ports to the gasket are within the realm of the backyard mechanic and result in a definite improvement in flow. TPI Specialties, Inc.

fers a unique box plenum setup—it looks great and is designed to increase high-rpm output without significantly reducing low-end power.

High-Performance Cylinder Heads

Another romanticized item is cylinder heads. In general, you'll find that the stock Chevrolet small-block head has a lot going for it because it is a good design. That is why the engine is still with us after almost forty years. Before you rush out and spend some of your hard-earned money for a new set of cylinder heads, there are certain facts you should consider.

Do you really need a set of better flowing heads? The stock 305/350 is designed to provide excellent driveability and output in the 2500-4500rpm range. The camshaft, intake system, and cylinder heads all complement each other in this rpm range. Once you have removed the restrictions in the intake tract and opened up the exhaust system, you still have to change camshafts in order to take full advantage of the stock cylinder head. There is no point in installing better flowing cylinder heads until you have done all this. Only once you have maximized flow through the stock cylinder heads should you begin to think of cylinder head modifications or cylinder head replacement.

The least expensive road to higher flowing cylinder heads is to have your stock heads ported. You can achieve noticeable results by having the intake ports matched to the intake gasket and having the same thing done to the exhaust ports. The intake and exhaust valve guide bosses are also on the large side and should be reduced in size.

Another modification that will yield beneficial results is to grind away the ridge that is left by the factory's machining operations beneath the valve seats. By grinding away this ridge, flow isn't impeded.

These modifications, along with a good three-angle valve job, will increase flow but you'll get better results when you opt for new cylinder heads.

When you're looking at cylinder heads, there are a few more things you should keep in mind. Some performance heads aren't cast with integral EGR (exhaust gas recirculation) passages or a heat riser passage. This passage is located in the center of the cylinder head and its main function is to provide quick warmup on carbureted applications. The passage runs underneath the carburetor mounting area. Installing heads without a heat riser on a street engine isn't recommended. Late-model cylinder heads come with raised valve cover rails and use central valve cover hold-down bolts—which means if you installed these heads on earlier engines you'll also need new valve covers.

Stock valve size is 1.94x1.50in intake and exhaust. Most performance heads will have 2.02x1.60in valves or larger. The 2.02x1.60in valve has been the standard valve size on the factory high-performance small-blocks and it is also the standard size on most factory performance heads. Going beyond the 2.02x1.60in valves is necessary only on competition engines; there is no point in getting more valve area than you'll need.

From the cylinder head chart it is easy to see that all the stock heads could be improved upon, but also remember that more flow doesn't necessarily translate into more usable power. One head may flow more than another at any given valve lift, but the key thing to remember is that the flow figures don't tell you how the head actually performs on a street car. Yes, there's more flow, but is that at the expense of flow velocity? Sacrificing flow velocity for more flow capacity is similar to installing an oversize carburetor.

SLP Engineering's high-performance aluminum heads replaced the stock heads here and feature 2.055x1.60in intake/exhaust valves. The intake and exhaust ports and bowl areas are hand finished and the heads come with a three-angle valve job. SLP Engineering, Inc.

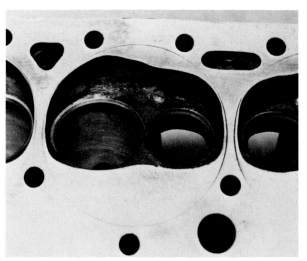

The combustion chamber on this Brodix race head has been reworked to maximize flow. The exhaust port is raised (as compared to a stock head), which allows for better flow.

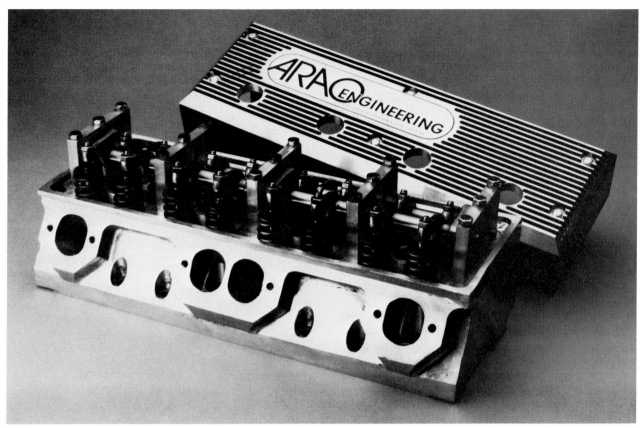

You can only do so much with the stock two-valve-per-cylinder configuration. To get more air in and out of the engine you need more valves. The aluminum Arao four-valve head for the small-block is designed to use stock type intake and exhaust manifolds, and the rockers are actu- *ated by the stock pushrods. More valve area also allows for softer valve springs and short-duration cam timing. Provided your engine's bottom end can take it, these heads will go to 9000rpm. Arao Engineering Inc.*

One more thing you should do is try to keep things in perspective in relation to cylinder heads. The stock Chevrolet head is a very good piece, especially when you compare it to the Ford 302 heads. The stock 302 Windsor head flows around 158/126cfm intake/exhaust at 0.600in lift while the GT-40 heads are somewhat better at 183/144cfm. It is only with aftermarket heads that flow levels begin to approach even a stock Chevy head. Mustang GTs run well in spite of poor cylinder head design. Dramatic gains in power, then, are to be found first by cleaning up the intake and exhaust system, along with installing a better camshaft and electronics.

If you can afford the additional expense, get a set of heads for your Camaro or Firebird that are cast in aluminum. The 50lb or so weight savings will improve handling.

There is always an "ultimate" cylinder head and in this case it is an aluminum thirty-two-valve head manufactured by Arao Engineering Incorporated. The Arao cylinder head has four valves per cylinder—two intake, measuring 1.6in, and two exhaust valves, each measuring 1.3in. The interesting thing about this

Raising the fuel pressure on the Chevrolet TPI system has produced power improvements as well as better throttle response. This particular unit is adjustable and is from TPI Specialties. TPI Specialties, Inc.

If you remove the throttle body on the stock TPI plenum, you'll see these two casting protrusions. These should be ground down for improved airflow. TPI Specialties, Inc.

head is that it is designed to work with the stock camshaft and pushrods. Both intake and both exhaust valves are actuated by a single pushrod from the stock location. Each rocker consists of two valve levers and one pushrod lever. Because of the additional valve area, the Arao heads will outflow any currently available head at any lift and rpm and they fit the 305/350 block with a minimum of alterations. The heads are also designed to work with currently available intake and exhaust manifolding.

Fuel Injection Conversion Kits

There are several fuel injection conversion kits currently available for carbureted Camaros and Firebirds. Best known is Holley's Pro-Jection universal fuel injection conversion, which provided improved driveability, throttle response, fuel economy, and increased power. This retrofit throttle body system designed for noncomputerized engines is made in several configurations. For a street engine, there is Model 3200, #502-2, which flows 670cfm. It is a two-barrel system designed for engines under 360ci and can sustain a 320hp output. Model 3400, #504-1, is a 900cfm four-barrel system designed for V-8 engines that produce between 300 and 600hp. Both require a four-barrel intake manifold and both kits come with the following:
- Dual 80lb/hr Holley-designed fuel injectors (four with #504-1)
- Adjustable fuel pressure regulator
- Electronic control module (ECM)
- Inline fuel pump
- Wiring harness

- Adjustable fast-idle solenoid

The electronic control unit (ECU) is user-adjustable to provide air-fuel settings for the choke, accelerator pump, and for power output at various rpm ranges. Besides requiring a four-barrel intake manifold, a return fuel line is necessary but otherwise it is a simple bolt-on installation. Naturally, a high-performance intake manifold will provide the same sort of power gains as it does with a carburetor. Holley's tests have shown that this system is good for 2-3mpg (miles per gallon) gain and about 0.50-0.75 second quicker in the quarter mile over a comparable carburetor.

For the all-out racer, Holley offers throttle body systems that flow up to 4,400cfm.

Digital Fuel Injection also has a throttle body system that works on the small-block. It uses GM throttle body bodies and along with a computer, the system comes with an oxygen sensor. The oxygen sensor is used to maximize fuel economy. The system is more complex than Holley's, but it is completely tuneable with a User Interface Module in which the fuel mixture can be adjusted at idle and at WOT. The unit can also be custom calibrated with Digital's CALMAP calibration software. You'll need an IBM-compatible computer to do this.

Another throttle body system that is more of a variation on a theme, is an EFI system made by Cuttler Systems. It uses a throttle body only for air induction, with individual injectors located at each port on a conventional X-type single-plane manifold. Electronic control is provided by a Haltech manage-

57

ment system that can be tailored to any application via a personal computer.

Ram Air Systems and Air Cleaners

Although it sounds like a great idea, a ram air system where a scoop is used to channel air into the intake system doesn't result in a large increase in power. There is a 1.2 percent increase at 100mph (miles per hour), 2.7 percent at 150mph, and 4.8 percent at 200mph. So you have to be moving very fast in order to see any gains from ram air. Thus, technically cars do produce more power with a ram air system and this can easily be verified on the drag strip. But it isn't due to ram air; rather, it's due to the fact that the air fed into the intake system is considerably cooler (denser) than the underhood air.

Typically, the air entering the carb has been heated by passing through the radiator and over the hot engine. An engine taking in hot air will produce considerably less power than one taking in cold air. For every 7.2 degrees in temperature drop the engine will produce 1 percent more horsepower. Thus if the outside temperature is 70 degrees, the underhood temperature 150 degrees, and the engine producing 300hp with underhood air, it will produce 345hp with outside air, assuming the fuel mixture is adjusted (enriched) to compensate for the cooler air.

Even lowly 2.5 liter powered Camaros and Firebirds have a flexible hose attached to the air cleaner which feeds the carburetor cooler, outside air. Therefore cold air systems should never be disconnected, but should be made more efficient and less restrictive. That is why the SLP cold air kit is such a good addition on any V-8 equipped TPI engine.

Carbureted and throttle body engines use conventional air cleaners. Their first priority is to quiet intake noise. The stock air cleaner used on the base 305s has been a single-snorkel, while two snorkels are used on the high-output carbureted engines. Still, the air cleaner has to be one of the most restrictive made (see photo). All you have to do is take the lid off to see how restricted it is. You can remove all those parts for better flow and use the two-snorkel system on engines not originally equipped with it. The best system would be one that combines the benefits of the stock fresh air intake with the effects of an air cleaner that uses a larger, less restrictive air filter element.

Horsepower Output on Three Induction Systems

RPM	Stock TPI	Holley 750 & Weiand Team G Intake Manifold (hp)	TPI Specialties Mini-Ram
2000	120.6	115.9	116.0
2250	137.6	131.3	132.0
2500	155.5	147.0	149.8
2750	181.3	162.4	169.7
3000	200.5	179.8	189.4
3250	216.1	194.1	210.0
3500	226.4	208.5	229.6
3750	232.6	223.3	243.7
4000	238.5	240.1	259.0
4250	242.3	256.8	274.8
4500	241.3	270.7	288.3
4750	231.5	279.3	300.2
5000	222.2	284.8	303.5
5250	216.1	285.6	311.5

Note: Engine is a stock 350 Corvette with 1^7/8in dyno headers.

Chart courtesy TPI Specialties, Inc.

Chapter 4

Camshaft and Valvetrain

With the rough idle a hot cam makes, you're letting the world know that you mean business. Still, it takes a lot of work to make a hot cam work in a street car. You can get a lot of horsepower from your engine by refining the stock intake and exhaust systems—and that may be enough so you won't have to sacrifice any of the stock camshaft's beneficial qualities such as driveability and mileage. Changing the camshaft will alter performance and affect the intake and exhaust system, relative economy, and driveability of your Camaro or Firebird. It is not something to be taken lightly, and choosing the wrong camshaft will not only result in a poorly running street Camaro or Firebird, but will also create additional work to get the car back into proper running street condition.

The stock cam found in most Chevrolet engines was designed for smoothness and low-end power to provide long, trouble-free performance. Changing to a performance cam will move the power-producing band up the rpm range of the engine. The problem

with selecting a cam is to figure out how far to move up the power curve without hurting low-end performance and mileage. Your goal should be to choose a cam that will increase power over stock without losing the economy of a stock cam. So how much power should a cam change provide? A good target is an increase of about 10 percent.

Two areas in cam design affect the engine's power curve: lift and duration. A cam with more valve lift will generally produce more power than a cam with less lift. However, there are practical mechanical limits to increasing the amount of lift. For street use it is around 0.500in. Anything more than that has a tendency to accelerate valvetrain component wear. Once you go beyond 0.500in lift along with high-duration figures, the only way to minimize lobe and valvetrain wear is to use a roller lifter camshaft.

Duration is the length of time, measured in degrees, that the valves are left open to allow the fuel mixture to enter and leave the combustion chamber. Obviously the longer the duration, the more mixture that enters and the more power the engine will

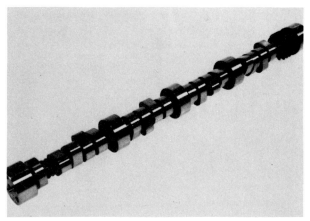

Roller camshaft and roller hydraulic lifters, by themselves, are worth an extra 30hp due to reduced frictional losses. They are stock on the 1987 and later 305/350 engines. Because the camshaft is made from steel, a steel distributor drive gear is required if you decide to use a roller cam in a pre-1987 block. Otherwise, the stock gear will quickly wear out. This is a performance hydraulic roller camshaft from SLP. SLP Engineering, Inc.

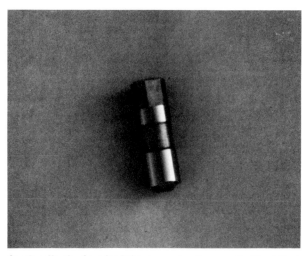

Stock roller hydraulic lifters require the use of a block that has machined lifter bosses. You can use regular flat tappet lifters on a roller lifter block, but you can't use the stock hydraulic roller lifters on pre-1987 blocks. Of course, you can use aftermarket hydraulic lifters for pre-1987 blocks.

Aftermarket hydraulic lifters are the way to go on any street engine and even on some competition engines. These are from Competition Cams. Competition Cams, Inc.

produce. Beyond a certain point, however, longer duration will mean more power but at the expense of low-end performance. The duration of a given cam is only optimized at a certain rpm or rpm range. If the intake valve opens at top dead center (TDC) of the intake stroke, by the time the column of air-fuel mixture in the intake tract gets moving to enter the cylinder, the piston will already be on its way down. The fuel mixture is always lagging behind. Thus the intake valve has to be opened earlier, especially as the engine revs faster.

Not only that, the valvetrain can't open the valve instantaneously and what is even more amazing is that the whole intake stroke process takes only 0.01sec at 3000rpm. At 6000rpm, the fuel mixture is lagging even further behind. To get complete—or more complete—cylinder filling at that rpm, the valve would still have to be open when the piston is on its way up during the compression stroke—which obviously it can't. That is why race cams have lots of

Most camshaft manufacturers recommend replacing the stock factory valvetrain components with new, stronger pieces when installing a new camshaft. This is definitely the way to go on a high-revving small-block, but it may not be necessary on an engine that will only occasionally see

6000rpm. This kit from Crower contains a new hydraulic roller cam, hydraulic roller lifters, dual springs with dampener, and new pushrods and spring retainers. Crower Cams & Equipment Co.

duration to increase cylinder filling, but that long duration kills the low-end. The thing to do, therefore, is to find a cam that combines reasonably high lift with duration short enough to allow good low-end performance.

Also remember that the current crop of computer-controlled cars aren't programmed to run with long-duration camshafts. The computer will only tolerate cams that have slightly more duration than stock. So unless you want to invest in an aftermarket (expensive) electronic control system, you're limited to using a stock or close to stock cam—but that isn't at all bad.

Also consider overlap and its effect. The overlap period occurs when both the intake and exhaust valve are open at the same time. It would seem that by having both valves open at the same time, the intake mixture would get diluted, thereby diminishing power output. However, if the exhaust valve is left open as after the piston has passed TDC (and the intake valve is opening), the exhaust gases will continue to flow out anyway and their flow will actually help to pull in more intake mixture. Like duration, a camshaft has to be designed to take advantage of this overlap period and like duration, the more overlap, the higher the rpm you need to turn the engine to take advantage of it.

You can determine overlap by a cam's lobe center angle which is the distance, in degrees, between the centers of the intake and exhaust valves. The greater the angle, the less overlap. A street cam can have angles in the 112 to 120 degree range. The stock 305/350 camshafts fit squarely in this category as they have a 115 degree angle. A smaller lobe center angle

A low-budget cam exchange should at the minimum include new lifters. Manley Performance

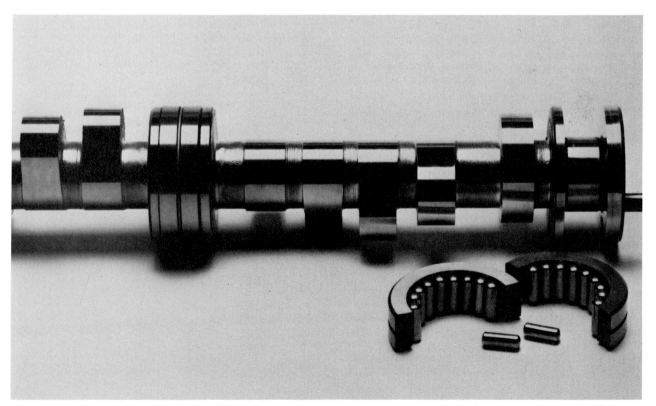

The reason Chevrolet went to roller lifters is greater efficiency. The same applies to the stock cam bearings. Crower has a special camshaft that utilizes needle bear- *ings and the result is less internal friction. This can translate to up to a 40lb-ft increase.* Crower Cams & Equipment Co.

will produce more top-rpm power while a higher lobe center angle will produce a better idle and a wider power band at the expense of some high-rpm power.

Most aftermarket cam manufacturers have a wide selection of cams that can also provide more lift with duration figures similar to stock GM cams. They also have hotter cams that increase duration in small incremental steps. Each manufacturer lists in its catalog what is best for your particular application according to the modifications already made on your engine. Remember that the hotter the cam, the greater the necessity of complementing that cam with the rest of the engine—meaning larger carburetor, exhaust headers, and so on.

With GM now measuring camshaft duration at lash point and at 0.050in tappet lift to describe cam events, it is easy to compare cams with those offered by aftermarket manufacturers as they measure at 0.050in lift. A practical limit for street operation is duration figures in the 230–240 degree range (measured at 0.050in lift). See the nearby chart for details.

Duration at 0.050in

Cam Lift (deg)	RPM Range
200	1000–4000
210	1300–4500
220	1500–5500
230	2300–6000
240	3000–7000
250	3800–7500
260	4200–8000

Hydraulic Roller Cams

High-performance engines in the 1960s usually came with a mechanical or solid lifter camshaft. Today there is really no point in choosing a mechanical lifter camshaft over a hydraulic cam. A hydraulic cam is maintenance free and easier on the valvetrain. Anti-pump-up hydraulic lifters can provide a top rpm of 7000 or so, more than enough for the street. A major innovation, as far as camshafts go, occurred on 1987 and later small-block engines. They came with

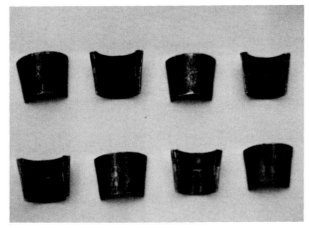

Anytime you remove the valves, you should always replace the valve keepers. These small parts can make all the difference.

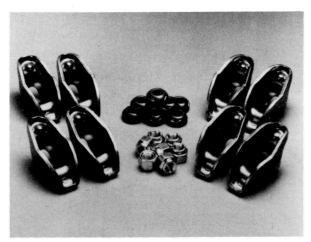

The small-block has used stamped steel rocker arms from the very beginning. These are both strong and cheap. Although the stock rocker ratio is 1.50:1, you'll find a great degree of inaccuracy with stock rockers measuring less than 1.50:1. A common modification is to use 1.60:1 rockers which translate into more camshaft lift. These are 1.60:1 stock type rockers with grooved rocker balls and self-locking nuts. The slots on these rockers have also been machined larger to eliminate any possible interference problems with the rocker stud. Don't forget to install valve springs that are 10 percent stiffer when going from 1.50 to 1.60:1 ratio. Manley Performance

In a high-output, high-rpm application, stud-mounted roller rockers are the way to go. These rockers reduce side loading to the valves which results in reduced valve guide wear, especially important when heavy valve springs are used. They are available from many sources. TPI Specialties, Inc.

hydraulic roller lifters. Previously, roller lifter camshafts were pretty much a race-only occurrence.

The advent of the hydraulic roller lifter combines the benefits of a roller lifter with the lack of maintenance of a hydraulic lifter. Roller lifters roll over the cam lobes which means they are much more reliable in high-speed, high-load applications. Roller lifters also enable the cam grinder to design cams with very high lifts and fast-opening ramps—qualities lacking in the stock 305/350 roller cam. However, roller lifters also reduce internal friction, thereby making additional horsepower. The roller cam used in the 305/350 is worth 30hp more than the comparable flat tappet hydraulic cam used in previous years.

The roller camshaft is made from steel rather than the typical cast iron used on flat tappet hydraulic and solid lifter cams, so it is more expensive. In addition, the stock roller cam can only be used on special 1987 and later cylinder blocks that are machined to accept hydraulic roller lifters. The stock hydraulic roller lifters are 0.63in longer than regular lifters and also require shorter pushrods, lifter guides,

and guide retainers. The camshaft also uses a thrust plate. You can use regular flat tappets with a roller lifter block but you can't use the hydraulic roller lifters on a regular block, at least with the stock roller lifters. And don't forget to switch your distributor's drive gear to a steel gear (see chapter 6 on electronics and ignition systems), otherwise the stock gear will quickly wear away—unless, of course, you install a camshaft that has a cast-iron gear pressed on.

The stock 1987 350 roller cam has an advertised duration of 294/294 degrees and 0.403x0.415in lift—a fairly tame grind. Duration at 0.050in lift is only 202/206 degrees. Listed in the GM Performance Parts catalog is one other hydraulic roller camshaft, part number 10134334. This is the same cam that is supplied with the 5.7 liter High Output over-the-counter engine. Duration at 0.050in is 235/235deg with 0.480in lift using stock 1.5:1 rockers.

Consult your favorite camshaft manufacturer for other additional grinds. There are many possibilities and your choice is dependent on what you do to the rest of your engine. The goal for a hot street car should be to maximize output without resorting to electronic modifications to your car's ECM (electronic control module).

Similar to the stock rocker in design, Competition Cams' Magnum roller rocker uses a roller tip with a stock type rocker ball. They are a good choice for a street engine. Competition Cams, Inc.

These rockers made from stainless steel are about as strong as you can get in a stud-mounted rocker arm design. Competition Cams, Inc.

Roller Rocker Arms

The use of roller rocker arms is another area often romanticized. They look great, even though you can't see them once the valve covers are bolted on, and they are a definite plus when it comes to high-lift performance camshafts because they will reduce side-to-side valve stem and guide wear. More often than not, you'll see a horsepower increase with aftermarket rockers simply because they are made to closer tolerances. Stock 1.50:1 rockers typically will have less than the specified ratio, which means less valve lift.

The small-block Chevrolet engine has used stamped-steel rocker arms since its inception. They are light, strong, reliable, and adjustable. If you aren't modifying your engine with a high-lift camshaft, there is no need to replace the stock rockers.

If you *must* have roller rockers, you can use aluminum roller rockers that are available from many sources and are a direct replacement for the stock rockers.

The stock rocker arm ratio is 1.50:1, meaning that the rocker arm multiplies the cam lobe lift by a 1.50 factor. Thus a cam with a 0.300in cam lobe lift has a

Stock valve springs are 1.25in wide. When you install a high-lift cam, stiffer than stock valve springs are usually called for. Since they are wider than stock, the valve seats on the cylinder heads will have to be machined to enlarge the spring pockets. Competition Cams' conical springs can be used on a hot street engine without resorting to machining. They measure 1.25in on the bottom and 1.46in at the top. Competition Cams, Inc.

Shaft-mounted roller rockers maintain valvetrain stability in an all-out racing application. Nice to have, but this is a bit of overkill for a street machine. TPI Specialties, Inc.

Steel spring seats must be used on aluminum heads, otherwise the springs will quickly chew up the head where they meet.

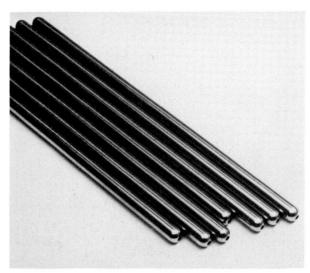

Don't forget the pushrods when installing high-pressure springs. One good shift and you'll be hearing noises in your engine unless you have pushrods that won't bend. These are Hi-Tech racing pushrods from Competition Cams. Competition Cams, Inc.

valve lift of 0.450in. A 1.60:1 rocker will provide 0.480in of lift at the valve on the same cam. Going from a 1.50 to 1.60 rocker ratio, though, will reduce the rpm at which the valves float. To maintain the same valve float speed, you must increase valve spring pressure by 10 percent. Still, switching over to 1.60 ratio rocker arms is a good, relatively inexpensive way to get some more power—10–15hp—from your engine. Going beyond a 1.60 ratio can be expensive and will most likely require different pushrods in order to maintain correct geometry.

Be aware, also, that you may have to enlarge the pushrod guide slots that are cast in the cylinder head with larger than stock 1.50:1 ratio rockers. The pushrod may hit the end of the slot because the pushrod seat on the rocker arm is moved closer to the stud in order to obtain the larger ratio. Naturally, you'll have to take the heads off.

Another modification that is useful on a high-performance engine is to replace the stock pressed-in rocker studs with screw-in studs. The stud bosses have to be tapped and milled for this. You can use either $^3/_8$in screw-in studs or go for big-block $^7/_{16}$in studs. The thicker studs minimize rocker arm flex under high rpm, but will require other than stock rocker arms.

The stock spring retainers are a one-piece design. These are fine for a street engine and for some race applications. However, never use aluminum or even anodized aluminum valve spring retainers on the street, unless you don't mind having bits of aluminum circulating with the engine oil. The valve springs can chew up the retainer. Stay with steel retainers, which are good enough to 7500rpm. Even though they are heavier, they are far more reliable and their slight weight disadvantage is of little consequence on a street engine. If you are installing a high-lift cam, you may also need shorter pushrods to maintain correct rocker arm geometry. Make sure to

ask the cam manufacturer; and always follow their recommendations when it comes to valve springs.

A final point concerns timing chains. If your 305/350 has a nylon timing gear, be sure to replace it. Although it is lighter and quieter, its reliability is questionable in a performance engine. A full roller timing chain and sprocket is best, but at the very least use a timing chain that uses iron gears.

Valves

Go ahead and install a larger carburetor or a performance fuel injection manifold and a hotter cam, but if the valves in your engine aren't big enough to let all that extra mixture in and out, it's a waste of money. The stock 305/350 cylinder head, however, has fairly decent size valves, measuring 1.94x1.50in intake/exhaust. Unless you are going for a very high power application, the stock valves are sufficient. The 5.71 liter HO engine available from GM Performance Parts, for example, uses aluminum heads with 1.94x1.50in valves and puts out 345hp.

You can install larger 2.02x1.60in valves that are readily available and that are common on most Chevrolet high-performance heads. One consequence of larger valves is that the valves will be closer to the combustion chamber walls which shroud the valves and thus restrict flow. In order to take advantage of larger valves, the combustion chamber will have to be modified by enlarging it to remove restrictions around the valves. This will result in a lower compression ratio. Also remember that in order to run unleaded gas, the stock valve seats were induction

It's fairly easy to follow the cam manufacturer's installation instructions and install the camshaft without any problems. By "degreeing" the camshaft you can be absolutely sure of its specs as installed. This degreeing kit is offered by Hi-Performance Consultants. Hi-Performance Consultants

Always replace the stock timing gear/chain with a roller type for maximum reliability. Wolverine Gear & Parts Co.

hardened. You'll either have to install hardened valve inserts or use a lead additive, otherwise the valve seats will quickly wear away. Considering the cost of new valves and the seat inserts, you may be better off getting a set of Chevy or aftermarket heads. Everything you do in an engine is a trade-off—you just can't get away from it.

Valve Springs

While the camshaft's lobes open the valves, it is the springs that close them—and this has to be done just as precisely and accurately. Rev an engine too high and the inertia effect on the valve springs may be too much so that the lifters won't be able to follow the cam lobe's contour. The result is valve float. Besides making the valves float, such a condition leads to further weakening of the springs. A 10 percent loss in tension means that the valve springs should be replaced. But a more serious consequence to valve float is the real possibility of the valves "kissing" the pistons, even if you have clearance notches on the pistons.

Common sense would dictate that to cure this problem is to install very heavy springs. This will work, but at the expense of increased valvetrain wear. You also have to install stronger pushrods and roller rockers to ease the strain on the system. What is needed is the lightest tension spring that will get the job done—and in this case you must follow the cam manufacturer's recommendations.

Most high-performance springs consist of a spring with a counterwound inner damper coil. Racing camshaft kits will also include a smaller inner spring which enables the engine to rev higher.

To install heavier springs, the heads will require machining to reduce the size of the valve guide so that the inner spring will fit, and to increase the size of the valve spring seats to accommodate the spring's larger diameter.

Recommendations

Changing a cam should be attempted *only* after you have first optimized the intake and exhaust system of your Camaro or Firebird. Passing an emissions test as part of renewing your registration is becoming a requirement in more and more states each year. Too often, a new cam will make your engine fail.

If you opt for more lift and duration, find out from the cam manufacturer or supplier you're dealing with which cams will work with the stock ECM and PROM. You can only go so far with the stock electronics, so stick with their recommendations. Going beyond this will require an additional investment because your engine just won't run properly.

Chapter 5

The Exhaust System

Much has been written about exhaust systems, about different types of headers and mufflers, and the benefits of each. Unfortunately, ignorance still abounds when it comes to exhaust system dynamics, and much of what has been written only compounds the problem. The result is that most performance exhaust systems aren't delivering what their manufacturers claim. This, again unfortunately, also applies to exhaust system components for current F-bodies.

After all, aren't headers and the rest of the exhaust system there to reduce backpressure, allowing the really important power-producing parts of your engine to get on with their jobs? Nothing is ever so simple—the more you know, the more you'll realize how complex headers and exhaust tuning is. It is not just a matter of slapping on a set of headers and expecting miracles. In many cases, the installation of headers will do little to boost power.

Headers, like everything else in the engine, must be chosen with an understanding of how they work and how they'll complement the rest of your engine's components.

Headers

Through a process called scavenging, headers let spent gases increase an engine's output. Specifically, scavenging is a process where a fast-moving column of gases extracts gases from a cylinder. When the exhaust valve closes, the gases in the header tube don't stop, they keep moving—possessing consider-

Restrictions are obvious in the stock exhaust system with its single catalytic converter—it is really a single exhaust system. The dual catalytic converter system that has been used on some 350ci engines is better, but it still is a single exhaust system because both dump into one exhaust pipe. Exhaust system modifications have traditionally been the first area to attack in the search for more power. A free-flowing exhaust system lets the engine produce all the power it was designed to.

All F-body cars have used a single transverse muffler with single or dual outlets. The problem with installing a conventional dual-muffler, dual-exhaust system is the lack of ground clearance. Previous F-bodies could use such a system because there was space. Current thinking is to retain the single transverse muffler system, but to use large exhaust pipes or tailpipes with a free-flowing muffler.

able momentum. This movement creates a small vacuum (a lower pressure area) under the exhaust valve. When it's time for the exhaust valve to open again, this lower pressure area extracts or scavenges exhaust gases from the engine. As exhaust gas speed increases, so does the scavenging effect. This means that the header tubing size must be small enough to maintain high exhaust velocity, but at the same time large enough so as not to restrict the engine at high rpm.

Thus a header with the correct tube diameter will show higher mile-per-hour and lower elapsed times on the drag strip. On a street car, a performance increase will be seen throughout the rpm range. But if the tube diameter is larger than it should be you'll experience a power loss due to reduced exhaust gas velocity. In fact, tubing that is only 1/8in larger than it should be for a particular engine combination may not even improve a car's street performance! The same car will probably show an improvement on the drag strip as the header is disconnected from the rest of the exhaust system, but this will be due to reduced backpressure and not to header scavenging.

It's the old bigger is better thinking. Big exhaust tubes are *thought* to be better. Bigger is definitely not

better in this case, however. Enthusiasts have always warned of the results of choosing an oversize carburetor, but rarely with the same sort of urgency when it comes to headers. And the car companies are just as susceptible to that kind of thinking.

Another point to consider when it comes to tubing size, especially as it applies to the drag strip, is that a maximum power header is not necessarily the same as a maximum performance header. On the strip, you are looking for the highest average power output during the time spent going down the strip. Certainly a big tube header will produce more power at a higher rpm but when the rpm drop during shifting, there is a horsepower loss resulting from the diminishing exhaust velocities. With a smaller tube header, maximum output is less, but low- and mid-range power is higher because the smaller tubing encourages better scavenging. Looking at the graph, as long as Area A is smaller than Area B, the use of a smaller tube header will result in a faster car.

Another so-called truth you probably read about is that you'll have to enrich your fuel system on a carbureted application after installing headers. Did you ever ask yourself why? The only time you have to enrich the carburetor is if you've installed a header

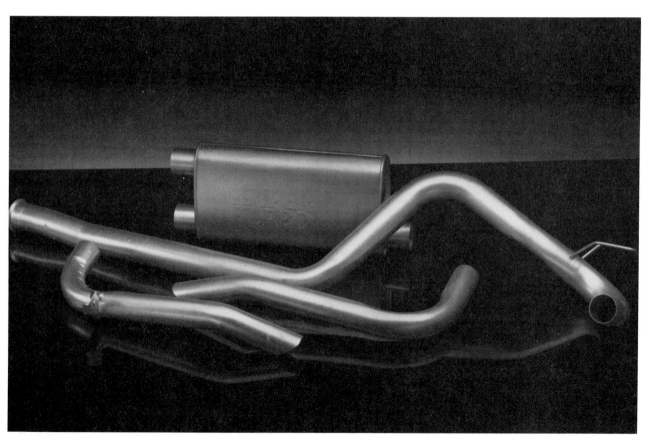

One of the least expensive ways to get more power is to replace the stock muffler and pipes. This is DynoMax's Super Turbo direct-fit system which is available for both dual-outlet opposite-side and dual-outlet same-side applications. The system uses Walker's highly efficient Super Turbo muffler. DynoMax, Div. of Walker Mfg.

with an oversize tube diameter. A larger tube diameter not only reduces gas velocity, but also the signal to your carburetor, thereby letting your engine run lean. A correctly sized header will not need this sort of adjustment and, in many cases, will actually cause the engine to run too rich. On fuel injected engines, the oxygen sensor will notice any variation in oxygen content in the exhaust and adjust the fuel mixture accordingly.

Thus on the street, big tube headers are of no value at all because they will reduce low- and mid-range output. At the top end, the restrictions inherent in the car's exhaust system nullify any advantage. And the same thing can occur on the track. An oversize tube diameter will only reduce overall performance.

If this is correct, why do many header manufacturers only sell headers with oversize tubes? Al-though some manufacturers list smaller tube headers in their catalogs, the sad truth is that customers want big tube headers because they believe that's the best way to go. Ever try to tell someone that his or her car will go faster with smaller headers? Old beliefs die hard.

How often have you heard that headers improve power by reducing or eliminating backpressure? Backpressure is another way of saying restriction. By following this logic, it would seem that a bigger header would eliminate backpressure. As we have just seen, this sort of thinking just doesn't apply with headers. It is far more applicable, however, when choosing mufflers and tailpipes, where large-diameter pipes and mufflers do make a difference.

Headers can also be "tuned" to help cylinder filling during the intake cycle. When the exhaust valve is open, a positive sound wave pulse is produced and travels to the end of the header tube. There it reflects back up the tube as a negative wave pulse. Assuming that the header tube length is correctly matched to the engine, the negative wave will reach the cylinder when both intake and exhaust valves are open (during overlap). As the negative wave collapses when reaching the cylinder, it reduces the pressure in the chamber, allowing more air-fuel mixture to enter —and thus creating more power.

The length of the header tube determines at which point in the rpm range the beneficial effects of exhaust tuning occur. The shorter the tube, the higher the rpm range where additional power will be made, and conversely, the longer the tube, the lower the rpm. To take full advantage of exhaust tuning, a manual transmission-equipped car should have header length that lets the headers tune at approximately the

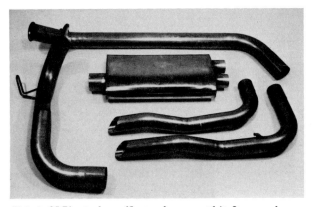

This is SLP's stock muffler replacement kit. It uses a larger 3in pipe from the catalytic converter (stock is either 2¼ or 2½in) along with a free-flowing muffler. Its high cost (it is made from stainless steel) is offset by its lifetime warranty. Both exhaust pipes exit on the driver's side.

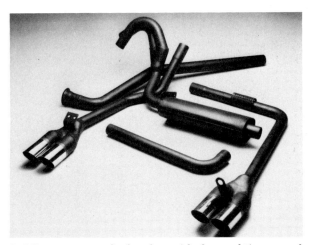

Dobi's system uses dual outlets with chromed tips on each side for a distinctive look. Dobi

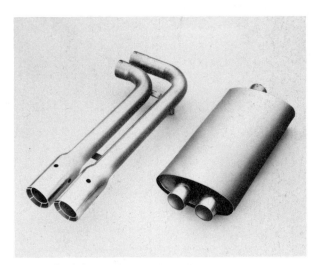

This is Borla's stainless steel muffler and tailpipes for the F-body. Borla mufflers are extremely efficient. The tail-pipes use Borla's intercooled round exhaust tips which are said to reduce backpressure for enhanced frequency quality. Borla Performance Industries

middle of the rpm range. An automatic-equipped car with the same engine should have header tubing that is 4 to 6in longer to boost lower and mid-range rpm which is important for an automatic on the drag strip.

If exhaust tuning is to be of any valve, the header tubes must be of equal length. If they are not, it will become difficult to properly tune an engine because the tube variations will cause one cylinder to run richer and another leaner. It is difficult to achieve perfection here, given the limitations of engine compartments, but for maximum power output, tube variation should not exceed plus or minus 1in. If a header is advertised to have a 36in tube length, all the tubes should at least measure between 35 and 37in. Problems will occur if tubing variation starts to exceed 1in, and if a header has a variation of 10in or more (some have as much as 21in!) the headers will show a negligible power improvement. Obviously, it will benefit you to install headers with equal-length tubes. A true equal-length header will run circles around a typical unequal-length header. Consider these dynamometer test results of a 355ci Chevrolet small-block compiled by Cottrell Racing Engines, Chaska, Minnesota. The engine was balanced and blueprinted, had a 9:1 compression ratio, a performance hydraulic camshaft, and highly modified cylinder heads. The intake system was the Chevrolet Tuned Port Injection system, which on one hand limited horsepower (with a 750 Holley, the engine put out 113 more hp!) but made the test fair, since the system is computer controlled. Both headers were tested with the computer making all the tuning adjustments.

The headers were $1^5/8$x36in Headers by Ed with tube length variation under $^1/4$in. The universal header was designed to fit Camaros, Chevelles, Novas, and so forth, with a $1^5/8$in tube diameter, but tube length variation was as much as $16^1/2$in. The shortest tube was 19in long while the longest measured $35^1/2$in. The results speak for themselves, with the Headers by Ed showing as much as a 31.1hp increase at 4500rpm.

Dynamometer Test Results

Engine RPM	Headers by Ed (hp)	Universal Header (hp)
2000	124.6	122.9
2250	143.4	144.3
2500	166.4	166.1
2750	195.6	193.0
3000	215.1	216.8
3250	235.3	239.2
3500	256.6	255.3
3750	278.6	270.3
4000	297.0	281.5
4250	310.0	286.7
4500	314.8	283.7
4750	303.3	280.4
5000	284.4	260.6
5250	270.5	257.6

Another point to consider is the collector. Most collectors measure between 4–12in, but 98 percent of the time, a longer collector produces more power. As much as 0.3sec reduction in elapsed time (ET) can be realized by the simple addition of a 12in collector.

The highly regarded Flowmaster muffler is a welded unit. According to many tests, the Flowmaster has made more power than a system that didn't use a muffler. Flowmaster Mufflers

This is because a collector creates a free-flowing secondary scavenging area.

For the person interested in more power the replacement of the stock manifolds is beneficial. The stock or mildly modified 305 does not respond well to tube diameters larger than 1½in, and you'll see a definite decrease in power. If you have modified your engine so that the car will run in the 12sec range or lower, then a 1⅝in tube or larger will be necessary, but a larger than 1½in tube will cause a power decrease in a modified 305 street engine. A 350 can tolerate headers with a 1⅝in diameter, but try to avoid the temptation to go to larger diameter pipes on a street engine.

Although there are several good headers that have equal-length tubes, most are suitable for racing only. One of the few manufacturers that offers an equal-length street header for the 305/350 is Hooker Industries Incorporated, under part number 2138. Tube diameter is 1½in, while length is 30in. Hooker made the 30in length specifically for a street type engine because the stock engine runs out of breath at around 5000rpm. The shorter tube length is designed to help the engine breathe better in this range. A 12in collector extension can be used to broaden the torque curve with these headers. The Hooker unit is a traditional four-into-one header with the left-side header connecting with the right side unit, thereby facilitating connection with the rest of the car's stock exhaust system. For a highly modified engine, Hooker offers a 1¾in tube diameter header; however, this is a traditional four-into-one design and does require separate exhaust pipes for each side.

SLP offers a 1⅝in system that is somewhat different in design. Their headers are of the Tri-Y design, which are set up to boost low- to mid-range torque—perfect for a street engine. They are made of stainless steel which makes them more expensive, but they have a lifetime warranty. The same system is available through GM Performance Parts.

Concerning legality, you'll find that most header manufacturers (as of this writing) are in the process of having their products certified for street-legal use. Look for certification when you shop.

No matter how good your headers are, most of the benefits they provide will be nullified if the spent gases have to go through the stock catalytic converters and mufflers, especially at higher rpm.

You can't judge a book by its cover and you can't judge a muffler by its looks. But you can at least look down each pipe to see if it necks down. If it does, it is creating restriction and that means less power. Thrush Performance

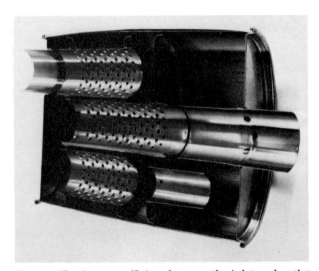

This muffler is more efficient because the inlet and outlet pipes do not neck down. On some cheapo mufflers that come in a variety of pipe diameter sizes, you'll find that they all use the same body with differing inlet and outlet pipes. It is better to have a large opening neck down to the pipe it is connected to than a larger pipe connecting to a smaller inlet. Thrush Inc.

Muffler design can vary greatly—the deflectors at each end channel the exhaust for better flow while the perforated tubes are designed to let the sound energy be dissipated into the fiberglass packing. American Industries Inc.

Stock Exhaust Manifolds

If you insist on using stock exhaust manifolds, the best ones to use on third-generation cars are the units that come on the L98 350ci V-8. The outlets on these manifolds measure 2.25in while manifolds used on 305 engines measure 1.87in. This will result in a small improvement, but nowhere near as much as with headers.

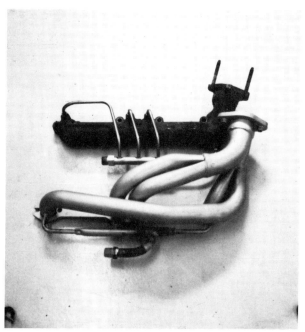

The stock exhaust manifolds (top) are extremely restrictive while the headers (bottom) are more effective. Their unequal-length design doesn't do much in the way of exhaust tuning. TPI Specialties, Inc.

Exhaust Pipes

As we have seen, headers are complex. It can be difficult to choose the right header that will work best with your particular combination, but the rest of your car's exhaust system is quite simple by comparison. Here, the bigger is better philosophy *does* work. The stock system's design, though, poses a problem, as it is in effect a single exhaust system. Both pipes from each exhaust manifold feed into a single exhaust pipe which contains the catalytic converter and then continues to the single transverse muffler that is common to all third-generation cars. The 1989 and later TPI engines came either with a dual converter setup which was optional or standard, depending on the engine-transmission combination. The dual converter exhaust system is an improvement, but it still dumps via a Y-pipe into a single exhaust pipe.

In an off-road race application you can achieve a good reduction in backpressure by using an exhaust pipe that eliminates the catalytic converter, assuming you are using the stock exhaust configuration.

Catalytic Converters

This brings us to the subject of catalytic converters. Catalytic converters are very effective in removing pollutants, but they have drawbacks. The biggest problem with converters is that they are restrictive. You can install aftermarket modified converters that increase flow, but be warned, they are expensive. Second, catalytic converters need to see exhaust gases that result from combustion of an air-fuel mixture in the 14.7:1 range, which is controlled by the engine's ECM computer. This is a fairly lean air-fuel ratio. If you've modified your fuel injectors or carburetor to provide a richer mixture for more power, then the effectiveness of the catalytic converter is greatly reduced.

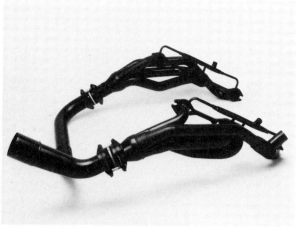

This type of header is available from Edelbrock. It is a well-made unit but like all shorty type headers, they don't provide much scavenging and unequal-length tubes limit output as well. Edelbrock Corp.

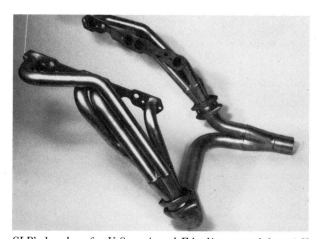

SLP's headers for V-8 equipped F-bodies are of the tri-Y design which boosts low- and mid-range output. Their stainless steel construction is somewhat more costly, but they have CARB (California Air Resources Board) approval and a lifetime guarantee. SLP Engineering, Inc.

Hooker offers two types of headers for 1982–92 F-bodies: a set that follows stock exhaust system configuration, and these which are the more common four-into-one design. These headers have 1³/₄in tubes and should only be used with highly modified engines. Hooker Industries Inc.

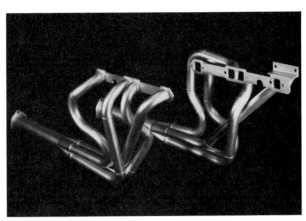

A smaller tube header may not produce as much horsepower at high rpm, but by producing more low- and mid-range power than a big tube header it will produce a higher average output, thus outperforming the big tube header on the strip. Note the extra-long collectors which boost low-end torque. Headers by Ed, Inc.

Another point to remember is that catalytic converters are extremely sensitive and over time, can clog up. A misfiring spark plug or the choke sticking in your carburetor in the morning is enough to make a converter useless. And as they get older, they clog. You'll often see cars that check out fine in terms of oil consumption, compression, emission systems, and the like, but are down on power. If they also tend to run hotter than normal, you can be sure that the cause is bad catalytic converters. This restriction in the exhaust system will cause burned exhaust valves and it can be particularly damaging to a turbocharged application as the extra heat will fry a turbocharger.

Mufflers

A final point to consider is mufflers. You can forget the stock mufflers because they are too restrictive. Stock mufflers are designed to meet noise regulations, while performance is a secondary consideration.

The muffler on the 305/350 engines has two outlets to simulate a dual exhaust system. About the only positive thing that can be said about the stock system is that it sounds nice.

Some may want to consider glasspack mufflers. These mufflers are a straight-through design which uses fiberglass to quiet exhaust noise. Made in various lengths (the longer, the quieter), there are important internal differences between different brands. The least restrictive are those that don't have the internal louvers protruding into the exhaust flow.

Glasspacks are hard to live with, however, and over the past fifteen years or so the big deal in street mufflers has been the so-called Turbo muffler. The original Turbo muffler was designed back in the early

1960s for use on the turbocharged Chevrolet Corvair. Many performance mufflers today still use the Turbo designation, as it is a name associated with performance.

Stock mufflers are necessarily restrictive because great restriction (which increases backpressure) creates a quieter unit. It follows, then, that lower restriction and backpressure will result in a more efficient muffler but at the expense of increased noise levels. The Turbo muffler is a conventional type muffler that uses absorption and reflection methods to reduce sound levels while maintaining low backpressure. Absorption techniques usually use a sound-absorbing material, most often fiberglass, to reduce sound energy, while reflection reduces sound energy by bouncing it off of internal baffles within the muffler. Most Turbo mufflers rely on reflection principles to reduce sound levels while others may use a combination of the two. Some well-known brands that fit in this category are Walker's Super Turbo, Thrush's CVX and Tough Truck Turbo, and the units available from Hooker and Hedman.

The Flowmaster muffler uses a noise cancelation principle that aims exhaust pulses at each other in order to reduce sound levels. Tests have also borne out the fact that the Flowmaster mufflers produce more power than with a straight pipe without any muffler. The AP XLerator muffler uses a system of perforations and passageways to dissipate noise. The mufflers made by Borla use several perforated pipes within the muffler that dissipate the sound onto stainless steel packing.

All of the mufflers mentioned here will provide considerably more power than the factory muffler; for example, the Flowmaster muffler by itself is good for a 15hp gain at the rear wheels.

Probably the easiest way to go is to replace the stock muffler with a high-performance unit in the stock location. The problem with a more conventional system that uses separate mufflers on each side is one of ground clearance and the added cost of fabricating new exhaust pipes from the headers and manifolds on back.

Exhaust Tuning and Superchargers/Turbochargers

If you've ever seen blown dragsters, you've probably noticed that they have very short straight or slightly curved exhaust pipes, called zoomies. There is no collector, and each exhaust port has its individual pipe. Because in a supercharged engine the supercharger force-feeds the cylinders, header scavenging is of no value at all—in fact, there is no header or exhaust scavenging in a supercharged engine. Therefore collector size, tube length, and tube diameter are of no importance in a supercharged engine. All you need to use is headers that are large and free flowing with a minimum of bends and restrictions. The same applies to the rest of the exhaust system. Large tubing and free-flowing mufflers are a *must*. You're dealing with a larger, hotter volume of exhaust gases and any restriction in the exhaust system is therefore amplified.

The nice part about an exhaust system is that after you've installed it, it requires little periodic maintenance and absolutely no tuning or adjustment. It just hangs there, letting you devote your time to other areas that require attention. It is easy to forget the exhaust system, and that's OK, but when you have the wrong combination, you can spend a lot of money and waste a lot of time trying to figure out what isn't working right when the real culprit is poorly chosen exhaust system components. Do some research, follow the guidelines described here, get the highest quality parts you can afford, and you'll know that the exhaust system is doing its part to increase your engine's output.

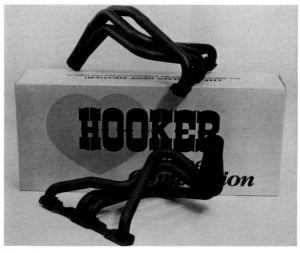

This is a set of Hooker's number 2138 headers for 305ci small-block equipped Camaros and Firebirds. It is an excellent choice for a street car because these headers feature a 1¹/₂in tube diameter and follow stock exhaust system routing. Hooker Industries, Inc.

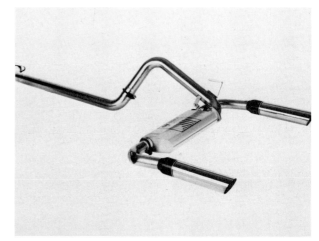

Thrush offers this CVX Power System for 1982–92 V-8 equipped Camaros and Firebirds. Designed to bolt on behind the stock catalytic converter, the system uses 3in diameter intermediate and over-the-axle pipes while the muffler uses dual 2¹/₂in diameter outlets. Thrush Performance Inc.

Chapter 6

Electronics and Ignition

By far, the least understood (and most misunderstood) system on the third-generation Camaros and Firebirds is the electronic computer control system which regulates all engine functions. The main reason for the increasingly complex computers and related systems is tougher emission standards. It is possible to design a brand-new "cleaner" engine in terms of emission output, but it is much cheaper to use an existing engine along with electronic management controls to keep emissions down to acceptable levels. The small-block engine was originally designed to provide a broad range of power with good fuel mileage and at a smooth idle. With the advent of emission controls in the 1970s, power output was compromised, as was driveability, idle quality, and fuel mileage as engineers concentrated on meeting emission requirements. However, the use of sophisticated electronic controls has enabled the small-block to meet emission standards while restoring horsepower output, mileage, and idle quality.

Electronic Engine Control Systems

All third- and fourth-generation Camaro and Firebird engines are electronically controlled, whether they are carbureted or fuel injected, and the system works in much the same manner in all engines. The system controls ignition timing, EGR (exhaust gas recirculation), and air pump flow. It consists of the main computer control unit, a series of sensors, and the engine's ignition system. The computer control unit is made up of two assemblies—the processor and the calibration assembly. The processor processes the information received from the various sensors, compares it to the values programmed in the calibration assembly, and then sends out signals to the ignition control box and actuator solenoids to adjust the system as needed.

The sensors measure intake manifold pressure, barometric pressure, water temperature, crankshaft position, throttle position, EGR valve position, air inlet temperature, and exhaust gas oxygen content. The oxygen sensor measures the amount of oxygen in the spent exhaust gases and from this information, the computer processor adjusts the carburetor's or fuel injection's air-fuel mixture, making sure that it is always within the calibrated parameters. On carbu-

reted engines, air-fuel adjustments are made through an electric stepper motor installed inside the carburetor. The distributor on these engines has no mechanical advance mechanism as all these functions are controlled by the electronic control module (ECM).

Let's look at the sensors used in current Camaros and Firebirds:

MAF—Mass Air Flow sensor: measures airflow in terms of mass (weight), which is independent of variables such as temperature, barometric pressure, and altitude.

ACT—Air Charge Temperature sensor: measures air temperature at the intake manifold.

BP—Barometric Pressure sensor: measures outside (atmospheric) barometric pressure.

MAP—Manifold Absolute Pressure sensor: measures the pressure inside the intake manifold on Speed Density and all TBI systems.

ECT—Engine Coolant Temperature sensor: measures engine coolant temperature. The ECM uses

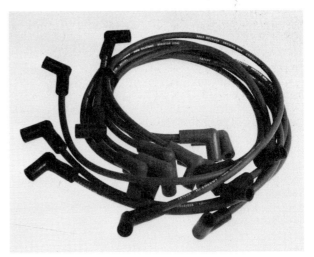

Your engine's ignition wires are often taken for granted. Even though the stock wires are 8mm thick, they are prone to failure. Use an aftermarket heli-core set that combines the advantages of a solid core with the resistance capacity of a resistor type wire. They are available from MSD, Accel, TPI Specialties, and many others.

engine coolant temperature as the basis for adjusting ignition timing and air-fuel ratio calculations. The ECM enriches the air-fuel mixture and advances timing several degrees to improve driveability when the engine is cold. This mode is in effect only at idle and at part throttle. As the engine warms up, the settings gradually revert to their normal positions.

TPS—Throttle Position Sensor: measures throttle position and according to the information it sends to the computer, the computer adjusts fuel flow and timing accordingly. Generally on V-6 and four-cylinder engines, at wide-open throttle the computer turns off the air conditioner (if so equipped) and the EGR valve, and maximizes fuel flow.

ISCV—Idle Speed Control Valve: regulates engine speed.

EGO—Exhaust Gas Oxygen sensor: measures air-fuel ratio. Located in the exhaust headpipe. If it is too high or low (rich or lean) the signal sent to the computer will enable it to adjust fuel flow back to factory specs. Disconnecting the sensor will make the computer go into richer open loop mode. This may or may not (probably not) make the engine run better.

Knock sensor: detects engine knock (detonation). The ECM then retards ignition timing until detonation ceases.

There are other sensors that regulate emission-related functions, again all controlled by the ECM unit. The ECM unit also controls when the lock-up converter engages in an automatic-equipped car.

Electronic Control Module (ECM) Operation

It is the electronic control module, or ECM, that is responsible for running the engine. Its primary functions are divided into three sections: the ROM, PROM, and RAM.

In the Read Only Memory (ROM) section, the basic calibrations or instructions are encoded for the computer to obey. These instructions are permanently stored in the unit and cannot be erased by turning off the power.

Most GM cars use the same basic ECM unit; it is through the PROM, Programmable Read Only Memory, where the ECM gets its specific instructions for the engine-transmission-axle combination it is installed in. The PROM is the one unit most enthusiasts are familiar with because it is through this unit that the ECM can be modified to produce more power. We'll look at PROMS later on.

The RAM, Random Access Memory, is the section where the ECM makes the mathematical calculations as the information from the various sensors comes in. It is here, also, where BLM or Block Learn Multiplier information is stored when the engine is running in open loop mode or when the engine is turned off. Also stored in the RAM are the diagnostic codes used to describe faults within the system. The familiar Check Engine light on the dash indicates problems in the system.

The electronic control module has nine modes of operation. The better known of these are open loop

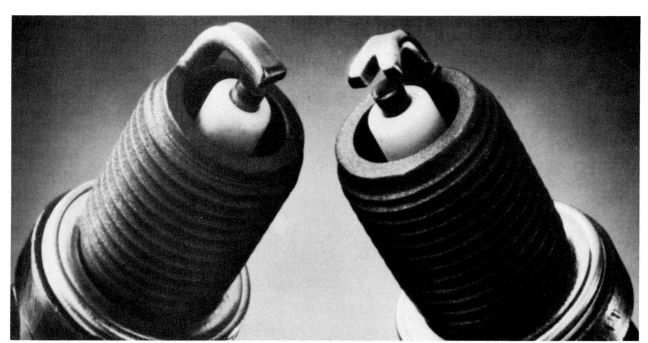

The Splitfire spark plug (right) has shown to be an effective aid in combustion chamber efficiency. The V-shaped electrode exposes the spark for better ignition *and more power, as has been borne out by tests. Splitfire, Inc.*

and closed loop operations, so we'll look at these first.

Open Loop

Open loop mode occurs when the engine is initially started and when the engine is at wide-open throttle. In this mode, the oxygen sensor's readings are disregarded by the ECM and the fuel system is instructed to provide richer than normal air-fuel ratios. This is primarily performed during initial start-up where a richer than normal mixture is required, and also at wide-open throttle where additional fuel is metered to maximize power output. In addition, at start-up, the ECM advances ignition timing.

Closed Loop

By utilizing the readings from the oxygen sensor, the ECM will maintain an ideal air-fuel ratio of 14.7:1 for best mileage and emissions. Closed loop mode is in operation during idle and part-throttle operation—in effect, the majority of the time the engine is running.

Limp Home Mode

The ECM goes into a limp home mode in the event there is a major sensor malfunction in the system. In this mode, the fuel curve is not set by the oxygen sensor and timing is set to about 22 degrees total.

Enrichment Mode

In this mode, the ECM enrichens the fuel mixture under certain conditions, which can be in either open or closed loop. In addition to wide-open throttle operation, enrichment occurs when the engine is under a heavy load, under high rpm, and when the engine is overheating. Extra fuel helps to cool the combustion chambers.

Leaning Mode

When the engine is operating under little or no load, the ECM will lean out the mixture beyond 14.7:1 to conserve fuel and reduce emissions.

Fuel Cutoff

All fuel going into the engine is shut off when the throttle is closed and the car is decelerating until rpm drops to below 1500rpm. This saves fuel.

Start-up

This is a special program that increases ignition timing and enriches the fuel mixture to ensure the engine starts and keeps running.

Clear Flood

You probably know that you aren't supposed to step on the pedal when you initially turn on a fuel injected engine. If you do depress the pedal more than 80 percent, the clear flood program is engaged which

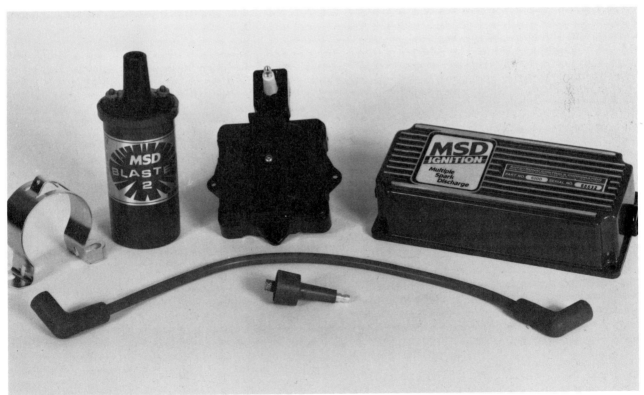

The MSD multi-spark system fires the plug up to twenty times, resulting in better ignition. This kit is designed for the GM HEI distributor and is a worthwhile addition. It comes with an externally mounted coil which is better than the stock GM coil. Autotronic Controls Corp.

either turns off the injectors or leans out the air-fuel mixture to about 20:1 so that the engine will start.

Aftermarket Chips

As can be deduced, it is difficult to fool the ECM system into enriching the fuel mixture and permitting more and quicker ignition advance. The best way to do this is to change the existing PROM chip. Fortunately, the General Motors ECM is designed for easy removal and replacement of the PROM unit.

On the Camaro and Firebird, the ECM unit is located behind the dash on the passenger side. After removing the unit, all you have to do is remove the access cover to expose the stock PROM chip, unplug it, and install a replacement chip. Most GM PROM chips use twenty-four-pin connectors; TPI (Tuned Port Injection) engines since 1986 use a sixty-six-pin connector.

Aftermarket replacement chips change the parameters by which the ECM operates by modifying the ignition advance curve and air-fuel ratio during open loop operation. Whereas the stock parameters are geared toward emissions and fuel economy, aftermarket PROMS are designed to increase performance. Most of these will almost always leave the stock closed loop values alone in order not to lose any fuel economy and driveability. Typically, a replacement chip on a stock engine will result in a $\frac{1}{4}$ to $\frac{1}{2}$sec improvement in the quarter mile. One of the better-known chip suppliers is Hypertech, and most aftermarket performance equipment suppliers offer replacement PROM chips as well. TPI Specialties carries an extensive line of PROM chips for the small-block Chevy engine.

A nice feature of replaceable PROM chips is that they can be specifically designed for a particular gear ratio, exhaust system, intake system, camshaft, and the like. In this way, a properly matched chip will enable the engine to produce the maximum amount of power possible.

On the other hand, a chip can't overcome any inherent restrictions that an engine may have—it can only maximize output from what you already have. In

This ready-to-run electronic distributor comes with mechanical and vacuum advance which is necessary should you decide to run your engine without the ECM computer. Autotronic Controls Corp.

Using an older style GM distributor, this kit includes MSD's Soft Touch rev limiter unit. With the Soft Touch rev limiter, you can set the maximum rpm at which you can rev the engine, from 5000 to 8000rpm, thereby eliminating the possibility of a ruined engine due to missed shifts. Autotronic Controls Corp.

On all 1982 and later ECM-controlled distributors, the ECM adjusts ignition advance. This kit from Mr. Gasket enables you to tailor the distributor's advance curve to your needs.

The PROM chip controls many of your engine's functions. Simply removing the stock PROM and replacing it with an aftermarket unit can result in a performance gain. Aftermarket PROMs are designed to work in conjunction with any other modifications you have made, so it isn't a matter of just plugging one in—each is tailor-made.

other words, it can't make any more power than your engine was designed to produce.

Once you go beyond the typical street modifications—headers, freer-flowing intake system, and a milder camshaft—you'll find that you've reached the limits of the stock ECM, even with aftermarket PROMs. The stock ECM cannot accommodate more radical camshafts or maximize output from highly modified engines. For those interested in maximum power output using electronic fuel injection, you'll need an aftermarket electronic control system that you can program for specific fuel and ignition curves. Accel/Digital Fuel Injection and Haltech Injection make systems that enable you to totally control all engine functions according to the usage intended. The need for such a system on the typical street car isn't necessary, but it is a necessity for the racer or the enthusiast who has a very highly modified car.

Ignition Modifications

As with all high-performance engines, you should make sure that your distributor cap and rotor are of the highest quality and also use the best spark plug wires that you can afford. The stock spark plug wires have a carbon core which not only has high resistance, but eventually breaks down. Solid core wires are the best in this respect, but unfortunately interfere with the car's radio and ECM computer. Your best bet is to purchase one of the many spiral core type wires available. These solid core wires offer little resistance and suppress magnetic interference.

Another modification that should be contemplated is replacing the stock coil. This can either be located in the distributor cap on 1982–86 5.0 liter engines, or remote mounted on 1987 and later V-8 engines. An aftermarket high-performance coil has a larger electrical reserve, which is necessary to fire the plugs on modified engines.

Engines would be best served with the addition of a multi-spark system, of which Autotronic Controls Corporation's MSD brand is the best known. During a firing cycle, rather than one spark, a series of sparks (usually up to twenty) is delivered to the spark plug and the results are obvious: much better combustion, noticeable improvement in idle quality, elimination of misfiring, the ability to fire fouled plugs, and more power. On engines with large, open combustion chamber designs, power can be improved as much as 4 percent. Another feature of the MSD system is that it can be used with MSD's Soft Touch rev limiter. The Soft Touch rev limiter cuts the spark to each cylinder and then fires it on the next cycle thereby preventing the engine from over-revving. The MSD unit can be purchased through the General

Adaptive Technologies has developed the Prompaq, a system that allows you to choose between four different PROM chips. In addition, the unit has a security chip that disables the computer when activated. The Prompaq unit is available for early and late (Prompaq II) style PROM chips. Adaptive Technologies

Motors Performance Parts catalog or directly through MSD.

Mounting an MSD unit is fairly easy. A good place to mount the control unit is on the inner fender apron next to the shock tower. The rest of the installation involves plugging the unit's wire harness into the stock wire harness. No cutting or splicing is required.

Although all ignition advance functions are now controlled by the ECM unit, you will find engines converted to pre-ECM specifications using an older distributor. In such engines, the centrifugal and vacuum advance units in the distributor control these functions. These can be adjusted for optimum performance.

Depending on engine timing, the spark plugs are fired a certain number of degrees before the piston reaches the top of its stroke. This is to give the fuel mixture a chance to ignite (as this is not instantaneous) and expand, and thus drive the piston down on its power stroke. At higher rpm, the fuel mixture still needs the same amount of time to ignite but because the engine is turning faster, the piston would be on its way down before the fuel mixture ignited. The spark advance mechanism in the distributor allows the spark timing to keep up with engine speed. This means that the spark has to be fired much earlier at higher rpm to compensate for engine speed. The centrifugal advance mechanism in the distributor advances the spark as engine speed increases, and retards it as speed decreases.

The rate of advance is controlled by two springs found underneath the rotor. By simply changing the springs to lighter ones, the engine will accelerate quicker, resulting in better throttle response and more low-end power. Mr. Gasket and others offer kits with different springs. A rule of thumb is to give the engine as much advance as it can tolerate without

pinging. This simple and inexpensive modification is highly recommended.

Pre-ECM-controlled distributors also have some form of vacuum advance—this is additional spark advance controlled by the engine's vacuum. When engine vacuum is high, such as when the car is cruising, the engine can tolerate more advance than the centrifugal advance provides. The result is better gas mileage. The vacuum canister should never be disconnected. Although most vacuum canisters aren't adjustable, they are interchangeable with canisters found in earlier models. (Consult a good repair manual for specs.) Aftermarket adjustable canisters, such as the one offered by Crane Cams, can easily be used.

Unless there is a good reason to switch to an older type distributor, you're better off using the stock ECM-controlled system. Aftermarket PROMs are calibrated to provide quick ignition advance which is also more reliable than a mechanical system. About the only other modification you may want to try is to advance initial timing by 2-4 degrees.

Distributor Gears

One final point concerns the distributor's drive gear. This is of importance if you are switching to a roller camshaft from a flat tappet hydraulic cam. Roller camshafts require the use of steel gears while regular flat tappet cam distributors come with a cast-iron gear. The cast-iron gear will quickly wear out with a roller cam. Bronze drive gears are usually recommended by aftermarket cam manufacturers and will work with either type of camshaft. However, as bronze is softer than cast iron or steel, it will wear at a faster rate.

On the other hand, you can use a steel roller camshaft that has a cast-iron gear. A cast-iron distributor drive gear can be pressed on the camshaft prior to final machining operations, thereby eliminating the need for a steel or bronze gear. If you are contemplating using a different camshaft, be sure to ask whether it is fitted with a cast-iron gear.

LT1 Ignition System

The 1993 LT1 engine uses a different ignition system than was used before. Instead of the traditional distributor mounted in the familiar position at the back of the block, starting in 1993 the LT1 distributor is mounted below and behind the water pump. The distributor is driven by a shaft from the camshaft sprocket which rotates a stainless steel shutter wheel. The shutter wheel has slots cut into it which enable an optical sensor to measure light that shines through the slots. The signals from the sensors eventually find their way to the ECM, which controls ignition firing. The system is supposed to be more efficient and because there is no distributor cap, it requires less maintenance. The LT1 is also equipped with platinum-tipped spark plugs that can last 60,000 miles.

Chapter 7

Supercharging, Turbocharging, and Nitrous Oxide Injection

No single engine modification will yield more power than will a supercharger. Without a doubt, it is the most effective way of boosting power. Chevrolet has shied away from turbocharging the small-block, although you will find turbocharged engines used in other GM cars. One particularly successful application has been the Buick V-6 which has found its way into an F-body, the 1989 Twenty-fifth Anniversary Edition Firebird Trans Am. The 231ci(3.8 liter) V-6 is turbocharged, intercooled, and uses electronic port fuel injection for a 250hp output. To date, it remains the fastest stock F-body, with low 13sec quarter-mile times and a top speed of over 150mph.

There are two types of engine superchargers. The first uses a belt-driven system, that is, one that is driven by the engine's crankshaft by means of belts, and is called a supercharger. The second type is exhaust driven and is known as a turbocharger.

If supercharging is so great, why isn't everyone doing it? First, supercharging is still considered to be

The only factory force-fed induction system came on the 1989 Twentieth Anniversary Edition Trans Am which used a turbocharged Buick 231ci V-6.

an "exotic" modification, meaning that the typical enthusiast doesn't know much about it. Second, supercharging is expensive. It often has been pointed out that when you add up the total cost of the usual modifications—new intake manifold, carburetor or fuel injectors, high-performance cylinder heads, hotter camshaft, and the like—the cost will be about the same as it would be to supercharge the engine from the beginning. This may be true, but the typical enthusiast usually modifies the engine piecemeal as the budget allows, but to supercharge an engine requires a fairly large initial expenditure, even for a mild application, say a unit with a boost of 5–7psi (pounds per square inch). And if you want to make a lot more power with higher boost pressures, you'll also have to get into the engine: new pistons and rods will almost always be required, in addition to other modifications and add-ons such as water injection and cooling system work. Supercharging your engine is expensive, but the results can be very satisfying.

Supercharging Defined

A supercharger is a device that forces more air-fuel mixture into the cylinders than the engine is able to draw in by itself. You may have heard of the concept of volumetric efficiency—for example, each cylinder of the 305 displaces 38.125ci of air when the piston is at bottom dead center (BDC). The force that fills the cylinder is atmospheric pressure, which is 14.7psi at sea level. If every time the piston went down and the cylinder was completely filled, you could say that the engine was running at 100 percent volumetric efficiency. Unfortunately this rarely happens when the engine is running—atmospheric pressure isn't enough to fill the cylinders completely. The typical 305/350ci V-8 engine as it leaves the factory is running at around 80 percent volumetric efficiency. The usual hot-rodding modifications—larger carburetors, high-rise intake manifold, exhaust headers, and so on—will improve this figure, but not to the 100 percent level.

Supercharging forces the air-fuel mixture in the cylinders to the point where 100 percent and even greater levels of volumetric efficiency can be attained. Restrictions that are eliminated in normally aspirated engines such as small valves, less than ideal intake and exhaust ports, a low-lift camshaft, and poor exhaust manifolds are much less of a problem in a supercharged engine. The air-fuel mixture is anxious to get into the cylinder in a supercharged engine because the intake manifold acts like a pressurized reservoir. The mixture is ready to rush into the cylinder as soon as the intake valve opens.

Supercharging also has the effect of increasing the effective compression ratio of the engine because a larger volume of air-fuel mixture is squeezed into the same space. Isn't that the same as using pop-up pistons? It is, but also remember that a supercharger forces the engine to operate at 100 percent volumetric efficiency. There is much more air-fuel mixture in the cylinder, which results in a bigger explo-

The Paxton supercharger has been around for a long time —since 1952. It is a blow-through design: all it does is force additional air through the intake tract. The supercharger can be installed in a day (or less) and it is legal for use in all fifty states. Paxton Superchargers

B&M's low-profile Roots type blower for the small-block Chevy. This particular application gets an additional kick from nitrous oxide injection. One of the advantages of a Roots type blower is its instantaneous response.

sion. For this reason, it is not recommended that the static compression ratio in an engine be above 9.0:1 as the supercharger will blow the engine apart because it will create very high cylinder pressures.

The major drawback that a supercharger has is that it increases the temperature of the air-fuel mixture—the temperature of any mixture rises as it is compressed. The higher the boost pressure, the higher the intake temperature. This can result in damaging detonation.

Belt-Driven Superchargers

There are many different types of superchargers. The most familiar one is the well-known GMC type which is used on dragsters. This is a Roots-type supercharger, most often referred to as a blower. This supercharger works much the same way as an engine's oil pump where two (or more) meshing rotors inside a housing compress the air-fuel mixture and force it on to the cylinders. It is a positive displacement supercharger, meaning that the volume of air that it moves is the same during each revolution the lobes turn. B&M Automotive Products makes such a blower specifically for the small-block Chevy engine. Roots type blowers are driven by a belt-pulley system connected to the engine's crankshaft.

Positive displacement superchargers provide instantaneous response—there is no lag for boost to build up.

Another supercharger type that enthusiasts are familiar with is the centrifugal type. Here an impeller, which looks like a fan, spins inside a housing. The air is accelerated by the spinning blades of the impeller. It is not a positive displacement supercharger because the amount of air flowing through it increases as the speed of the impeller increases. Thus, the impeller must spin at a very high speed in order to make

boost, and boost drops off at low speed. Most common is the Paxton supercharger, and like the Roots type blowers, it is belt driven.

Exhaust-Driven Turbochargers

Another type of centrifugal type supercharger is a turbocharger. Its main section is very much like the centrifugal supercharger; however, in a turbocharger, an additional impeller and housing is used, both sharing the same impeller shaft. Hot exhaust gas is used to spin this second impeller, thereby providing the motive power of the unit. The faster the engine turns, the more exhaust flow and the more boost the turbocharger makes.

Turbochargers have some disadvantages when compared to belt-driven superchargers. Because both impellers share the same shaft, a lot of heat is transferred to the intake tract, thereby reducing the turbo's efficiency. This can be alleviated by an intercooler—in effect, a radiator that is used to remove heat from the air entering the engine. Camshaft profile is also an important factor with a turbo; exhaust valve lift and duration have a direct bearing on how efficiently the turbocharger operates.

But probably the greatest drawback to a turbocharger is the problem of throttle lag. Because it

The Vortech is another centrifugal type supercharger. In standard form it puts out 5psi boost, but it can be adjusted for 11psi. According to Vortech, air inlet temperature is 40 degrees less than the Paxton and the unit is lubricated by an engine-fed oiling system. Vortech Engineering

Using the traditional GMC blower will require a very tall hood scoop or, as in this particular application, nothing at all. This Firebird does accelerate!

takes time for exhaust flow to build up when the throttle is floored in a turbo application, it therefore takes time for boost to build up. This can be minimized with careful design, but it is always present.

Draw-Through vs. Blow-Through Systems

There are only two ways a supercharger system can work. In a draw-through system, the supercharger is mounted in between the carburetor and intake manifold. The supercharger pulls or draws air-fuel mixture through the carburetor (or fuel injectors), compresses it, and sends it on to the intake ports. The Roots type blower is a draw-through system.

In a blow-through system, the carburetor (or fuel injectors) is mounted in between the supercharger and intake manifold. The supercharger pumps air (without any fuel) into the carburetor (or fuel injection air tract in the case of a TPI 305/350). The Paxton is a blow-through design.

Supercharger/Turbocharger Considerations

There is no point in installing a supercharger on a tired engine with loose rings and leaky valves. You're not going to realize much benefit and you'll just hasten the engine's demise.

A question that often comes up with force-feeding your engine is the amount of boost the typical engine can tolerate with no problems. A unit with a boost in the 5-7psi range is generally no problem for the stock 305/350 engine. The stock compression ratio is certainly low enough and the engine can tolerate an occasional burst to 6000rpm. This is considered a mild application. But boost in the 8-10psi range is definitely borderline for a street engine, and above 10psi you are on very shaky ground. In order for the engine to tolerate a lot of boost, the block and associated parts must be strong enough to withstand all that extra pressure.

The more power an engine makes, the more heat it will produce. In a mild-boost situation, the stock radiator should be fine but anything beyond that will require a larger radiator. It is easy to overlook the cooling system. In addition, you should switch to a good synthetic motor oil if you go this route. Synthetic oils tolerate higher engine heat and also have the ability to draw heat away from hot engine parts much quicker than regular oils (see the section on synthetic oil in chapter 14).

High heat also causes detonation. There are three things you can do to eliminate detonation: use a higher octane gasoline, reduce the compression ratio, or retard engine timing. In a mild-boost application, you may not have to do much beyond using the best gasoline available, but you may also have to retard timing. In addition, it is generally agreed that in a carbureted application, the carburetor must be enriched to the tune of 20–25 percent on the secondaries and about 10 percent on the primaries. Besides the fact that the engine will run better, the extra fuel acts as a coolant.

If you still encounter detonation, you should consider water injection. During a high-boost situa-

On carbureted applications, a carburetor enclosure is required with a Paxton Supercharger. The enclosure seals and pressurizes the carburetor inside and out; therefore, fuel pressure must be increased to exceed blower boost by 3psi, otherwise fuel won't flow into the carburetor's fuel bowl. The carburetor's jets must also be enriched. Follow the manufacturer's recommendations closely.

One of the most respected names when it comes to turbocharging the small-block Chevy is Gale Banks. This is the potent Banks dual turbo kit. By using dual Rajay/ RM turbos, turbo lag is minimized. And since it's a low-profile system, there is ample hood clearance. This setup is good for 500–800hp, depending on your engine configuration. Gale Banks Engineering

tion, a stream of water is injected into the air-fuel stream. The water vapor cools the cylinders enough to inhibit detonation. Water injection does not make more power, but rather permits the engine to run whereas before it would detonate—but only up to a certain point. Most manufacturers have water injection kits available.

Turbocharged applications can also benefit through the use of a knock sensor. The knock sensor will retard timing to a safe level if detonation is sensed. The TPI 305/350 engines already come with a knock sensor.

Some turbo manufacturers use a system that retards ignition advance under hard acceleration to avoid detonation. Again, it all depends on how much boost the system puts out.

The stock ignition system is sufficient to handle the spark requirements of a supercharged or turbocharged system. However, the addition of an MSD control unit along with high-quality spark plug wires and distributor cap and rotor is always recommended in a high-performance application.

It is logical to assume that if the stock camshaft works well in a supercharged or turbocharged application, then a high-performance camshaft with more duration and overlap would also work better because it would let even more air-fuel mixture in. This is not the case, however, because what works in a normally aspirated engine doesn't work in such an application. In a normally aspirated engine, when both the intake and exhaust valves are open, overlap is actually helpful as the fast-moving exhaust helps to draw fresh mixture into the combustion chamber. In a supercharged or turbocharged situation, there is no need for excessive overlap because the intake mixture is always under pressure, rushing to fill the cylinder as soon as the intake valve opens. If both valves open, all that happens is that some of the pressurized mixture is pushed out the exhaust valve.

When it comes to camshaft recommendations, most cam manufacturers simply recommend their RV cams for such applications. In fact, the stock 305/350 cam is fine. The only other recommendation is to have the entire cam advanced 2-4 degrees and if you still feel that you need an aftermarket cam, have one ground with a dual-pattern profile, emphasizing exhaust duration. The supercharger or turbocharger gets lots more air-fuel mixture into the cylinders and consequently, it does take more time to get all the burned exhaust gases out.

It would also be a good idea to install heavier intake valve springs as boost can hold the intake valves off their seats. An intake valve that hangs up in a supercharged carbureted engine is certain to spell disaster. The resulting backfire will most likely destroy the supercharger. But this isn't a problem on injected 305/350s, as all that is being pumped into the engine is more air.

It stands to reason that if the engine uses more air-fuel mixture, then you'll also need more fuel. It is

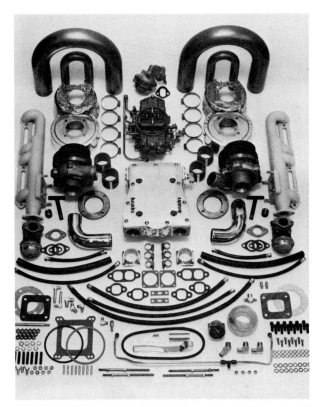

A turbo kit is more complicated than a supercharger and requires more time to install. To get all the benefits from the Gale Banks dual turbo kit, you'd also have to make other internal engine and driveline modifications because the stock components aren't designed for the tremendous boost in power. Gale Banks Engineering

best to follow the manufacturer's recommendations. Generally, you'll need more fuel volume and in some cases, more pressure as well. On carbureted engines using a draw-through system, a high-capacity mechanical fuel pump such as a Carter or a Holley should be sufficient. In blow-through systems you may also need more pressure as fuel pressure should always exceed blower pressure by 3psi. On EFI systems, install a higher flow electric pump, such as the Bosch pump offered by TPI Specialties. An adjustable fuel pressure regulator, such as the one available from TPI, is also recommended. You'll need about 100psi pressure on a system that has 10psi of boost.

If you are considering a high-boost system, you'll need to get into the engine since the stock pistons, rods, and block won't be able to handle the extra power. A four-bolt block is a *must*, as are heavy-duty rods with high-strength rod bolts and forged pistons. In addition, it is a good idea to have the block O-ringed, and use studs instead of head bolts. As with any high-performance engine, all specs should be blueprinted. Obviously, this is an expensive proposition, but if you want all the power that the small-block can produce, supercharging or turbocharging is the only way to go.

Recommendations

There are kits available in all supercharger configurations for the 305/350 engine. Roots type draw-through blowers are available from B&M, centrifugal blow-through superchargers are available from Paxton Superchargers and Vortech Engineering, and turbocharger kits are available from Gale Banks Engineering and many others.

Like any other engine modification, cost is an important factor when it comes to supercharging or turbocharging. In terms of cost, a Roots type blower, such as the B&M, is the least expensive and is particularly well suited for a carbureted application. Installation is not difficult. According to B&M, a mild 350ci V-8 using stock heads with 1.94x1.50in intake

and exhaust valves will be limited to under 400hp output. The limiting factor is the cylinder heads. For higher outputs, you'll need bigger heads. It seems that with whatever type of supercharger or turbocharger you use, it would pay to have freer-flowing heads.

For a fuel injected engine, a centrifugal type supercharger, such as the Vortech and Paxton, have several advantages including lower cost and ease of installation. At this writing, the Paxton also has a CARB exemption, making it legal for street use in all fifty states. You can expect about a 100–125hp increase with this type of supercharger and there are intercooler kits available to boost output even more, depending on the application. Once again, even minor porting will be extremely beneficial in terms of output.

The Roots and centrifugal type blowers, while providing a major increase in the horsepower depart-

You practically have to re-engineer your car when you opt for the massive increase in power that forced induction brings. The stock F-body driveline is barely adequate and has no built-in reserve as do late 1960s muscle cars. Of course, when you do go the whole route, you'll have transformed your Camaro or Firebird into one of the fastest cars on the road. Gale Banks Engineering

ment, are still considered a mild-boost application. For someone who wants all-out performance, turbocharging is the way to go. The financial commitment for the kit alone can be $3,000 and more for such add-ons as timing controls, bypass valves, and water injection. For really serious applications running over 10psi boost, you'll also need to get into the engine with new pistons, head work, and so on, so that the 305 and 350 will live. It all depends on how fast you want to go and how much you want to spend.

Nitrous Oxide Injection

Considering the amount of power you can get from a nitrous oxide system, it has to be rated highly among the modifications that you can make. However, it is also dangerous; it is easy to lose an engine by holding the gas pedal to the floor too long. Most nitrous oxide systems operate only when the gas pedal is floored.

If you remember, supercharging makes the intake mixture denser by compressing it so that more of it fills the combustion chamber. Nitrous oxide does the same thing, but by a different method. As the nitrous oxide gas decomposes, it releases the 36 percent or so of oxygen that it contains. By adding more fuel to this extra oxygen you have the makings of an instantaneous boost in horsepower. In addition, as the nitrous oxide changes from its liquid stored form to a gas, temperature drops, again creating a denser mixture. Still, there are problems. All that extra oxygen and fuel create a huge amount of heat in

the combustion chamber and thus cause detonation. For this reason, the amount of fuel that is injected along with the nitrous oxide gas is considerably more than required in order to keep temperatures down. If there is a malfunction in the system, combustion chamber and piston temperatures will hit stratospheric levels almost instantly, usually resulting in melted pistons. The same thing can also result if the nitrous is left on too long.

The typical nitrous oxide system consists of a tank of nitrous oxide, which can be stored in a convenient place such as the trunk. The pressure in the tank, 750psi, is enough to inject the gas into the intake manifold. An additional electric fuel pump is used to inject the additional fuel that is necessary. Both the nitrous gas and extra fuel are controlled by a pair of electrically operated solenoids which are normally connected to a switch that is activated only when the throttle is floored. How long a tank lasts depends on how efficient the system is, but 2-3min (minutes) is typical.

Of course, the ultimate system would be one that combines supercharging or turbocharging with nitrous oxide injection. If you're considering such a system, make sure you consult with someone who is familiar with such applications.

Used judiciously, a nitrous oxide system can provide a massive burst of power just when you need it.

This is Compucar's nitrous oxide system for the Chevrolet TPI system. It's what you'd call a basic system, as the nitrous is injected through a spacer plate that mounts behind the stock throttle body. Easy installation and a large power jolt are some of the positive aspects of nitrous oxide injection. Compucar Nitrous Oxide Systems

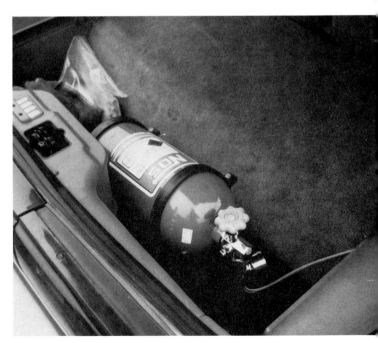

The nitrous bottle can be located in the hatch area of the typical F-body.

A more efficient system utilizes a line nest system that delivers fuel and nitrous oxide gas to each individual runner. The advantages include reduction of fuel separa-tion, more power, and, besides, they look great! Arizona Speed & Marine

Anytime you consider boost levels over 10psi, you should have the cylinder heads O-ringed to prevent head gasket failure. This nifty O-Ringer is available from Powerhouse Products. Powerhouse Products

Chapter 8

Transmission and Driveline

If you modify your engine for more power, you will invariably put more strain on the rest of your car's driveline, which consists of the transmission and rear axle. The first-generation Camaros and Firebirds had plenty of built-in reserve capacity in this area, but the third-generation cars we're addressing here weren't originally designed for the amount of torque that the current 305/350 engine pumps out. As the 305/350 has been gradually modified by the factory to put out more power, the transmission and rear end have been a source of problems for the enthusiast, but there are things that you can do to avoid trouble.

Manual Transmission

Initially, Camaros and Firebirds equipped with the 305ci V-8 came with either a Borg-Warner T10 or a Saginaw manual transmission—both four-speeds. The T10, which has been around since the 1960s, is fairly strong but the Saginaw can't really be considered a performance transmission because it is too weak. The T10, though, as installed in F-bodies, has several hindrances. It uses a twenty-seven-spline output shaft (vs. thirty-two for earlier GM-application T10s), and first gear is too low with a 3.27:1 ratio. You can use earlier T10 internals, but you can't swap a

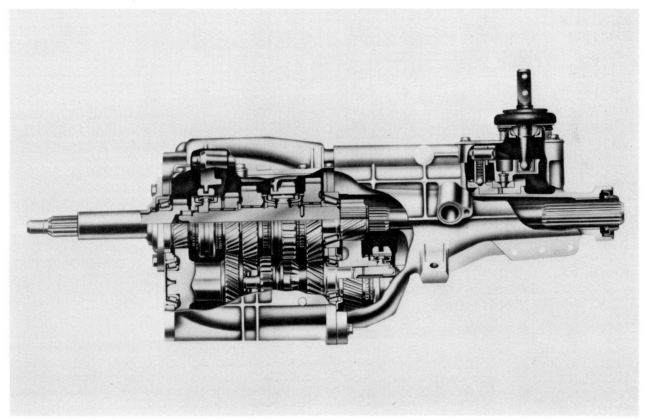

The World Class T5 five-speed manual transmission from Borg-Warner. When the transmission was originally designed, it wasn't intended for the 305's current torque

output. With a 305lb-ft torque capacity, the T5 is a marginal unit.

Powershifting causes stress cracks (arrow) which eventually result in broken gear teeth and transmission failure.
Steve Collison

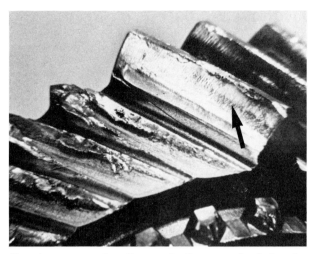

Gouging occurs when the gear teeth are overloaded as the mating gear tooth breaks through the oil's lubricating film. A synthetic fluid would stand up longer because it has higher film strength. Steve Collison

complete unit because of the different shifter location, no torque arm provision, and a different mainshaft speedometer gear location.

In 1983, F-body cars got the Borg-Warner T5 five-speed manual and even at that time when the 305 was putting out only 165hp, the T5 was considered to be a marginal transmission. Breakage was common, and although the transmission has been strengthened and torque handling capability increased over the years, it is still no match for the 305. The T5 has never been available with the 350ci V-8 engine. When the transmission was designed it was not envisioned that horsepower ratings would start rising again. It may be of some comfort to Camaro and Firebird owners that Mustang owners have exactly the same problems because they, too, use the T5.

If you own a 1982 car and want to move up to a T5, you'll need a 1983 T5 bellhousing (part number 14060627), T5 upper and lower supports (part numbers 14050111 and 14050112), and T5 console, shifter, and driveshaft. The reason you'll need 1983 parts is because the 1983 cars still used a mechanical clutch linkage which is the same as those found on the 1982s. From 1984 on, the bellhousing was redesigned to accept a hydraulic clutch release system.

Of course, the T5 can last the life of the car provided you don't beat it or powershift it. Powershifting is when you don't let off of the gas between shifts. You can say that *any* transmission has only so many powershifts in it before it fails, but it just happens that the T5 doesn't have very many. One powershift won't generally break a gear, but the cumulative effect of many powershifts will. High shock loads imparted during powershifting cause stress and fatigue cracks on the gear teeth until they eventually break off. This is especially so on the third gear.

Spalling can also occur on the pilot journal of the mainshaft (see photo). This occurs under severe use combined with poor lubrication under hard acceleration when high-G forces push the transmission oil to the rear. Spalling will continue to worsen, even under light loads, once it starts.

There are certain things you can do to help extend the life of your T5. First, use a quality synthetic transmission fluid such as Red Line's MTL. Synthetics have much higher film strength, can withstand heat better, reduce drag, and flow freely at very cold temperatures. Also change the fluid every 5,000 miles if you decide to stay with conventional fluids. And don't use hypoid gear lubes in the T5. They are too thick for the T-5's close tolerances and small oil passages. Gear lube is also not compatible with the fiber-lined blocking rings on T5s built since 1985.

It is also a good idea to install new shift fork pads whenever the transmission is opened up. They are inexpensive and tighten up sloppy shift forks. Speaking of shifting, the Hurst shifter for the T5 feels great and is recommended. It does create more noise, though, because it doesn't have rubber isolating it from the transmission as does the stock unit.

But, still, the best life extender for the T5 is not to powershift. And *never* powershift fifth gear, as most T5s will fail.

There have been two T5s available on the F-body—both close-ratio units with ratios of 2.95, 1.94, 1.34, 1.00, 0.63 (0.73 on 1983), and a stronger version from 1988 up which has more durable World Class inner workings. It has a 305lb-ft torque capacity, thanks to stronger syncros, tapered support bearings, and needle bearing mainshaft gears. Although it is a heavy-duty transmission, it too is not strong enough for the small-block V-8. It is possible to convert a regular T5 to World Class specs through the use of a new third-gear cluster and other modifications, but you're better off considering an aftermarket unit.

You can also fine tune the overdrive gear on your T5. Custom overdrive ratios are available from Char-Trends which allow you to have a 0.59, 0.63, 0.73, or 0.80 overdrive ratio on the T5.

If you baby your T5 it will last, but once you've modified your engine you're almost forced to at least consider an aftermarket transmission.

There are several ways to go here. Richmond Gear has the 4+1 five-speed manual. It is strong enough with a 450lb-ft torque capacity, but the fifth gear ratio is 1:00:1. Currently in the works, and due to be available by the time this book is out, is a six-speed overdrive version of the transmission. The Borg-Warner T56 is another six-speed that can be adapted for the F-body. SLP is also producing an installation kit for the Corvette ZF six-speed in the F-body (as they have done in the Firehawk). All of these transmissions require additional modifications in terms of bellhousings, cross-members, and even floor pans.

There is also the Tremec TR-3550 five-speed which so far has been available for 5.0 liter Mustangs. Future versions for use behind the small-block Chevy may be contemplated, provided there is enough demand.

The 1993 Z-28 and Trans Am are equipped with the Borg-Warner T56 six-speed manual. This transmission is strong enough to handle the torque output of the 350ci V-8. Two versions are currently available. Cars equipped with the standard 2.73:1 rear axle ratio are equipped with a T56 that has the following ratios: 3.36/2.07/1.35/1.00/0.80/0.62. With the optional 3.23:1 rear axle ratio, the first through third gear ratios are 2.97/2.07/1.43. Fourth, fifth, and sixth are the same.

Clutch and Pressure Plate

If you're going to drive your Camaro or Firebird hard you'll want to upgrade your clutch and pressure plate to withstand any additional power output from your engine. The first thing to consider is your flywheel. The stock flywheel is made from cast iron and it is adequate for high-performance use, provided you don't rev over 5000rpm. In a high-performance situation, the stock flywheel won't do at high engine speeds; you're risking the possibility of a flywheel explosion. So before you even consider what kind of

Inadequate lubrication and overloading cause spalling (arrow) on the pilot journal at the front of the input shaft. Once this starts, it will continue to get worse, even under light loads. Steve Collison

Replacing the shift fork pads (arrows) is a good idea whenever your T5 is apart. They'll tighten up the slack in the shift forks. Steve Collison

Rounded teeth on this third gear are also evidence of hard usage. Steve Collison

Powershifting and overloading will require the replacement of your T5 or its internals. Shown is the countershaft

cluster gear and third-speed gear for the World Class T5. It is possible to install these in a non-World Class box.

The old standby for improving acceleration is changing the rear axle gears. Changing rear axle gears has a profound effect on the way your Camaro or Firebird runs. Changing to a higher numerical ratio will improve acceleration but the engine will rev higher during cruising, thereby reducing mileage. Conversely, changing to a lower numerical ratio improves mileage at the expense of acceleration. You'll also have to change the speedometer gear in the transmission so that your speedometer will show correct miles per hour.

flywheel to buy, you should invest in a steel bellhousing, such as the one from Lakewood.

Performance flywheels are made from either high-strength steel or aluminum. A lighter flywheel made from aluminum lets the engine rev faster, once you get the car going, and is preferable in a road-racing situation. A heavier steel flywheel is recommended for street use as it holds more rotational inertia, allowing the car to accelerate faster from a standing start. These flywheels also have special frictional facings on the clutch side which complement a particular type of clutch.

A clutch disc consists of a splined hub that mates with the transmission's input shaft, an outer ring, and the lining material which can either be bonded or riveted. For street use, always use a clutch that has a cushioned hub. The cushioning effect is achieved by five small coil springs that are attached to the outer ring. The springs dampen the shock forces during engagement of the clutch. A race clutch disc will not have these springs thereby transmitting the shock to the rest of the driveline, and the facing materials are often designed to wear away quickly.

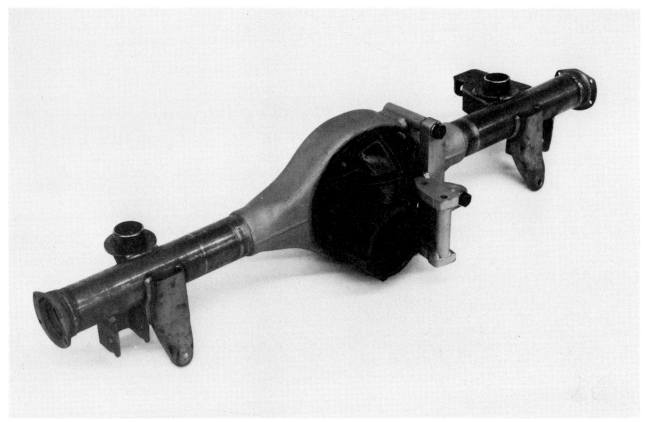

For maximum rear end durability, a 9in Ford is the way to go. This housing is from Moser Engineering Inc. and is a simple bolt-on installation. Moser Engineering Inc.

A street clutch usually has an organic or non-organic type lining which allows for a smooth engagement while some high-performance units use a metallic lining. Like metallic brakes, these need to be heated up a bit to grab properly, but they last considerably longer.

The biggest mistake you can make is to install a high-pressure pressure plate. This not only puts a strain on your left leg, but it also puts a lot of strain and increases wear on the clutch linkage. The stock pressure plate is a diaphragm type, which is easier to disengage than Long or Borg & Beck type pressure plates. Early diaphragm clutches had a reputation of hanging up between shifts, but the current units are reliable and dependable. Stick with a diaphragm clutch, but make sure to use quality parts.

The 1982–92 V-8 equipped Camaros and Firebirds came with a 10.4in clutch. Highly modified cars and those with nitrous or supercharging should use a heavy-duty clutch and pressure plate. The stock diaphragm pressure plate is made from cast iron, while high-performance units can be made from nodular iron or steel.

Automatic Transmission

Up to 1983, the automatic transmission used behind most Chevrolet engines was the TH200 three-

Although the 8.5in Dana 44 rear is strong, for all-out racing the old Ford 9in rear is stronger. The ones with the letter N on the case are made from stronger nodular iron. You might be able to find a used one at a salvage yard before a restorer gets to it first, but new assemblies are available from Motorsport. One advantage of the 9in rear is that the housing—the "pumpkin"—can easily be removed and replaced by another housing with a different gear ratio. Ford Motor Co.

speed. The TH700-R4, a four-speed overdrive unit with lock-up converter, became available in 1983.

Both of these transmissions were responsible for giving GM cars a poor quality image—transmission failure was common. Since the late 1980s, the R4 has been strengthened to the point of excellent reliability.

Of course, if you so desire, there are swap kits available from B&M and Gale Banks to enable you to install the older TH350 and TH400 GM automatics into the F-body. Both of these units are three-speeds, but it isn't really necessary to use one on the street considering how much more useful the overdrive ratio on the R4 is for a street car.

There are parts available from aftermarket suppliers to enhance the automatic's performance and reliability in high-horsepower applications. These include performance valve bodies, shift kits, anti-high-gear kick-down kits, and high-stall torque converters. You can even buy completely built-up units from such well-known suppliers as B&M, Art Carr Performance Transmission Products, Darrell Young Racing Transmissions, and SLP, to name a few.

A high-stall speed torque converter may be OK on the drag strip, but never use one on a street car. A converter that has a higher stall speed allows more slippage before it engages—it is like revving up the engine without engaging the clutch in a manual transmission. By allowing for more slippage, the engine produces more off-the-line acceleration. The drawback to a high-stall converter is poor fuel economy and a higher transmission fluid temperature. This can be quite detrimental to the transmission's life expectancy. Increasing transmission fluid temperature by just 10 percent can reduce the transmission's life by 50 percent.

About the only other thing you can do for your automatic is to install a transmission oil cooler. There are many available from aftermarket sources.

It is quite likely that anytime your engine overheats, your transmission fluid also will overheat since the stock fluid cooler is routed through the radiator. In such cases it would be wise to change transmission fluid as well, but typically it isn't done, reducing the life of the transmission. You should also use a synthetic transmission fluid.

Rear Axle

The rear axle used on the F-body is another driveline weak point. Over the years, General Motors has made some effort to strengthen the stock rear as horsepower ratings have gone up. But the reality is that the stock rear end is barely adequate for even stock use. If you've modified your engine for more

Another possibility is using a Chevrolet twelve-bolt rear instead of the stock rear. This is the Summers Brothers Z-28 rear end assembly and it is a bolt-on installation. Summers Brothers Inc.

One area where you can't afford to skimp is the rear axles.
Whatever rear you use, you should use the highest quality
axles you can afford. Moser Engineering Inc.

There is no part of the driveline that you can overlook once
you've modified your engine. A lightweight aluminum
driveshaft like this helps to overcome the rotating mass
inertia so the engine revs quicker. Tex Racing Enterprises,
Inc.

A Posi rear's advantages are made evident in bad, wet, icy
weather conditions as it allows the transfer of torque to the
opposite axle if there is slippage. It also improves acceleration. The Auburn locking differentials use cones instead
of clutch plates and have been used in F-body rears since
1985. Auburn Gear Inc.

A quality clutch is necessary for any high-performance application—not only to ensure that the engine's power is transmitted to the rear wheels, but also for safety's sake. Stock cast-iron components aren't reliable under hard usage at engine speeds over 5000rpm. The Centerforce clutch system from Midway Industries has a centrifugal assist feature which provides 30 percent more holding capacity than the stock clutch while maintaining stock pedal feel. Midway Industries, Inc.

power, it is inevitable that you'll have to replace the rear sooner or later, if you drive hard. Unfortunately, the fourth-generation cars continue to use the same rear axle.

Two types of rears have been used on the F-body. The more common, which is identified with a ten-bolt cover, is the Saginaw rear. This unit has seen service in many other GM cars. Initially, it came with a 7.50in diameter ring gear but in 1985, it was upgraded to a 7.625in diameter. The extra 0.125in helps, but it doesn't make a big difference. The axle shafts were also upgraded in 1990 to twenty-eight-spline units from the twenty-six-spline units used on earlier cars.

Also available is a nine-bolt-cover rear axle made by Borg-Warner. This unit is standard with certain high-performance F-body applications, such as the Twenty-fifth Anniversary Edition Trans Am. It has a slightly larger 7.75in ring diameter, and its axle shafts are held in place by bearing retainer plates rather than the C-clips used on the Saginaw rear. Summers Brothers Incorporated offers a C-clip eliminator kit that minimizes the chance of wheel loss in the event of axle breakage.

The Dana 44, with its 8.5in ring gear, was at one time available through GM. Although it has been

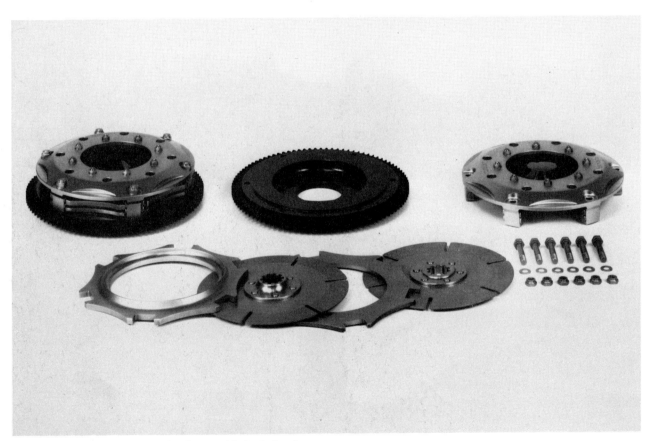

For all-out racing, this Tilton clutch assembly includes the very best components—flywheel, discs, and pressure plate. Tilton Engineering Inc.

discontinued, it is now currently available from SLP. The Dana 44 is designed to accept late-model (1989–92) rear disc brake calipers and mounts, and the stock torque arm and control arms bolt up with no modifications. Axle ratio availability from SLP includes 3.31, 3.54, 3.92, and 4.09:1.

In terms of other aftermarket sources, according to Summers Brothers, the best rear to get is the Ford 9in. It is the strongest and has the greatest axle ratio availability, but its shortcomings include high cost and a slightly greater power loss than other rears due to the fact that the pinion gear centerline is very low relative to the centerline of the ring gear. If you do decide on a Ford rear, use one for a full-size passenger car with 3.25in diameter tubes and 3.150in inside diameter housing ends. This housing is slightly heavier than the intermediate car housing, but it is substantially stronger. Do not use twenty-eight-spline axles or Lincoln units with a $9^3/8$in diameter ring gear because there are no aftermarket race parts available. Ford rears are available from several sources, including Moser Engineering Incorporated, Currie Enterprises, and Summers Brothers.

In terms of strength, the Dana 60 rates second after the Ford unit, but it does have its shortcomings. It is a very heavy unit and gear changes are more difficult because the center section isn't removable as is the Ford unit.

You can also use a twelve-bolt Chevrolet rear axle that has been modified to fit the F-body. Camaro and Chevelle units are difficult to find, but you can use a twelve-bolt rear from an Impala or Biscayne. Race parts are available from Summers Brothers.

The advantages of Tilton's Super Starter are many: it provides 50 percent more torque than original equipment starters, has ball bearing construction, is smaller, and weighs only 10lb. Tilton Engineering Inc.

On the street, a steel bellhousing is a good idea because it can withstand a clutch explosion—something the stock bellhousing cannot do. This one is from Lakewood. Mr. Gasket Co.

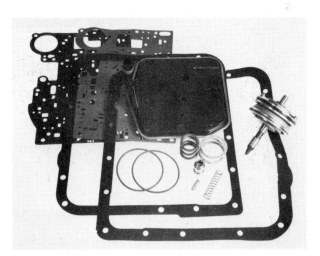

SLP's Shift Recalibration Kit is a must if your car is equipped with the 700-R4 automatic transmission. It improves shift quality by firming up the shift points. By reducing the overlap period when the transmission is in two gears during an upshift, the transmission's reliability is improved. SLP Engineering, Inc.

SLP's high-stall speed lock-up converter raises stall speed by about 800rpm while retaining the converter's lock-up feature for good fuel economy. The result is faster acceleration. SLP Engineering, Inc.

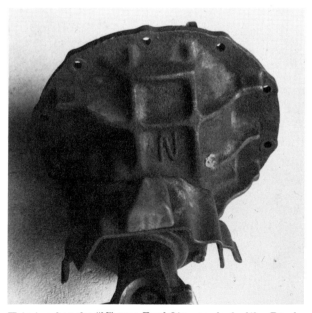

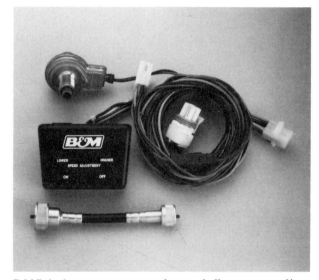

B&M's lock-up converter speed control allows you to adjust the speed at which lock-up occurs. This eliminates converter lock or unlock cycling. B&M Automotive Products

If you have an open rear end, installing a Posi type differential is recommended for improved acceleration. A Posi differential is a limited-slip type differential which divides torque between the two axles. If one wheel loses traction, the clutch assembly inside the unit disengages and the torque is transferred to the other axle. In an open rear the car would just sit, with one wheel slipping. The Auburn cone-type differential is a limited-slip type unit that has

The Richmond four-into-one five-speed has more than enough torque handling capability for most high-output small-block engines. Fifth gear, though, is a 1:1 ratio. However, a six-speed version that has an overdrive sixth gear will be available shortly. Regal-Beloit Corp.

This is what the "N" case Ford 9in rear looks like. Randy Ream

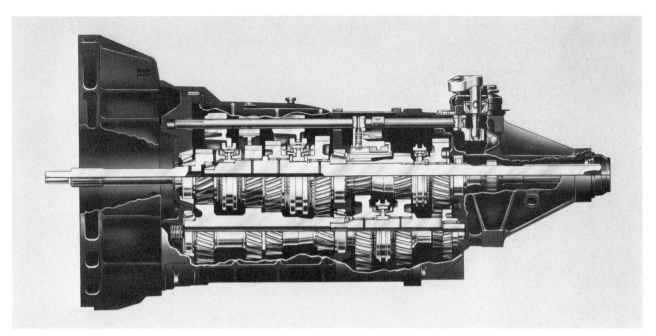

The reason that the 5.7 liter engines on the fourth-generation F-body cars can now be optioned with a manual transmission is the availability of the Borg-Warner T56 six-speed manual transmission. It features overdrive fifth and sixth gears, an integral shift rail system and constant mesh synchronized reverse. Chevrolet Motor Div.

The T56 is strong enough to handle the LT1's output with its beefy internals. It has a 450lb-ft torque rating. Chevrolet Motor Div.

been used from the factory since 1985 and is the one to use on earlier cars.

Axle ratio selection depends on how you are planning to use your car. With the advent of overdrive transmissions, choosing a high numerical axle ratio won't negatively affect mileage as badly as it used to with older performance Camaros and Firebirds. However, one point to keep in mind is when you change gears on the ten-bolt Saginaw rear, if you are changing from a 3.08:1 ratio or lower to a 3.23:1 or higher (and vice versa), you'll also have to swap axle housings because of ring gear thickness difference. The 7.5in and 7.625in ring gear sets are interchangeable in earlier and later housings, but some pre-1985 non-Auburn Posi rears may not clear the larger 7.625in gears.

As with any other mechanical part that requires lubrication, use a synthetic lubricant rather than conventional lubricants in your rear axle.

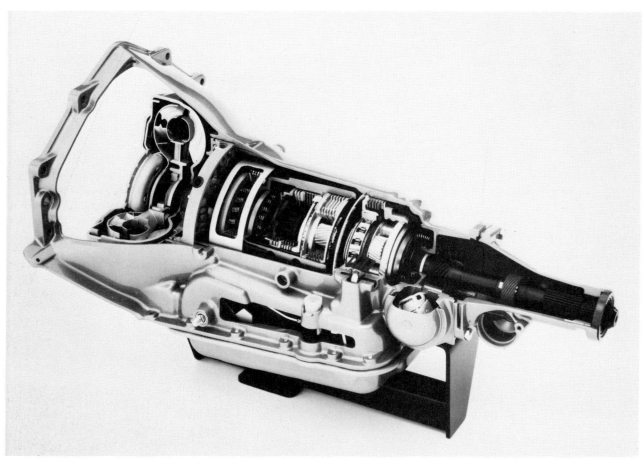

1993 Firebirds and Camaros have the Hydra-matic 4L60 four-speed automatic overdrive as optional equipment. It has excellent torque handling capability, but for hard usage, an external transmission oil cooler is a good idea. Chevrolet Motor Div.

Chapter 9

Handling and Suspension

In the good old 1960s, performance meant one thing: straightline acceleration. Handling was more of an afterthought. There were the smooth-handling Z-28 Camaros, of course, but they were a distinct minority. However, third-generation F-bodies are better balanced automobiles because of the current emphasis on handling.

During the 1980s, Detroit finally realized that while handling meant a safer car, handling could sell more cars. Not only do third-generation F-bodies handle better than earlier F-bodies, but engine development has progressed to the point that current cars are faster than most late 1960s hot-shots. The result is a much more satisfying Camaro or Firebird.

Handling is a vast and sometimes complicated subject that can encompass a lot of different things, but it all really boils down to one thing: traction. I don't mean traction during cornering; handling involves all facets of driving—during acceleration, braking, and cornering under all types of conditions and on different types of road surfaces. Good handling means control and predictability. A Camaro or Firebird that is handling well is a blast to drive while one that doesn't handle well will not only be difficult to drive, it will also be unsafe and even dangerous.

Camaros and Firebirds have always been designed with performance in mind. Third-generation cars are engineered to handle better than previous versions, but with most enthusiasts, there is always room for improvement. The guidelines given here are aimed at preserving a balance among the qualities that constitute good handling while maintaining a reasonable ride. The enthusiast who is concerned with performance is usually willing to give up some ride quality, but it is unwise to go overboard and sacrifice driveability and comfort.

There are some differences in suspension design on the third-generation F-bodies from the previous two. The front suspension, which previously used a double wishbone system, was replaced by a MacPherson strut front suspension. A MacPherson strut system is simpler (meaning less expensive) because rather than using an upper control arm, a tube is attached to the top of the front hub, extending to the top of the spring tower. Inside this tube is a damper

and the tube also acts as the seat for the front springs. Since the front hub assembly can only pivot on the lower attaching arm, the front wheel's up-and-down motion is on an arc. Weak front struts will invariably result in inner tire wear. On the F-body, rather than having the springs mounted around the damper, they are located on the lower control arm and the cross-member.

On the rear, coil springs replaced the leaf springs. Rear axle location was determined by two locating links, one on each side below the axle and a track bar (Panhard rod) mounted on the right rear part of the axle and on the top left of the body structure.

The fourth-generation F-body cars reverted to short and long control arm front suspension, which is similar in concept to the suspension used on the first- and second-generation cars. The reasons given are reduced friction and better ride. Also new on fourth-generation models is the use of a rack and pinion steering system, replacing the previous recirculating ball system.

Handling boils down to one thing—traction. In order to have good handling you have to eliminate or at least minimize all the dynamic forces that try to keep the tires from doing their job. This Camaro exhibits some lean which tends to lift the driver's-side front wheel, thereby limiting the speed at which the corner can be taken. Dennis Ashlok/Firestone

101

Understeer and Oversteer

Probably the most important terms to know and understand when it comes to handling are understeer and oversteer. All F-bodies are designed to understeer. This means when your car approaches and enters a turn it would rather continue going straight (because of centrifugal force). Enter a turn too fast

This particular Camaro isn't what you would consider to be the best choice for autocrossing in a stock class. Because it is a base Camaro, the chassis is loose, the springs are soft, and the tires are too small—all contributing to slow lap times.

This stock Trans Am exhibits less lean because the suspension is firmer, thereby allowing the tires to do their job. The result is better handling and faster lap times. Once everything has been equalized in terms of tires, springs, antisway bars, and so on, driver skill is the difference between winning and losing.

and the car's front end will start to slide, and turning the steering wheel more will not do any good; the only thing you can do is slow down and turn the wheel away from the turn. Most manufacturers consider understeering preferable because simply by following your natural driver's instinct you can still control the car and save yourself from spinning out.

In an oversteering situation, the opposite occurs. Because the rear tires slide out first, the car will continue turning tighter relative to steering input. Deliberate suspension design and rear weight bias cause this. If not corrected, the car continues making a tighter turn and at the limit of adhesion, the car will spin to the inside. Slight oversteer is preferred in racing because a skilled driver can control the car more easily and corner faster.

With most rear-wheel-drive cars you can also induce what is called power oversteer in a turn by stepping on the gas, assuming you have enough traction and horsepower.

Driving a car that understeers excessively is no fun at all. A Z-28 or a Trans Am or any other F-body with performance suspension components will still understeer, but much less. You can reduce understeer by adding oversteer via these methods: (1) increase front tire and wheel size; (2) stiffen the rear springs; (3) increase front tire pressure; and (4) increase rear stabilizer bar diameter (or add one).

Springs

All third-generation F-bodies have coil springs at all four corners. Installing firmer springs is an easy way to improve handling, however, you should leave springs for last because you are better off if you can improve handling without resorting to firmer springs. Firm springs will make you aware of how many rattles your car has and can take a lot of the fun out of

Drag racing calls for a different kind of handling. A looser, softer sprung front end will aid rear weight transfer and therefore traction as the car leaves the starting line. One thing you can do to help weight transfer is to temporarily disconnect the front antisway bar.

driving. There are suspension kits that provide every-thing you need to transform your car's suspension, and these usually include springs. These springs typically will also lower your Camaro or Firebird's ride height. Handling is no doubt improved, but you are compromising your car's ride and losing ground clearance which is not recommended. After all, it's no fun having your oil pan "kiss" the ground. See how your car handles after you've installed better shocks, tires, and stabilizer bars and then see if it's worth swapping springs.

If you have a non-high-performance Camaro or Firebird, you can upgrade the stock springs by switching over to comparable Z-28 or Trans Am springs that are available. A Z-28 or Trans Am has very good handling (in terms of skidpad g rates) from the factory, but even a stock car has a very firm ride. You can get firmer springs from several sources, such as Herb Adams, Global West, and Guldstrand Engi-neering, but then again, it all depends on whose handling philosophy you follow. For example, Guldstrand recommends upgrading the front springs by 30 percent and lowering the rears by 22 percent for cars used in slalom and autocross competition but, again, these springs have to be used with specific rear antisway bars to make the combination work.

The 1982–92 F-bodies have a MacPherson front suspen-sion. The strut is attached to the hub and to the top of the shock tower, pivoting only on the lower control arm. Front suspension travel is not straight up and down, but on an arc. The spring mounts in between the lower control arm and chassis.

Rear suspension uses coil springs and is located by two control arms mounted underneath the axle housing and

track bar (Panhard rod) attached to the left side of the axle and the body structure.

Shocks

Shock absorbers control the up-and-down movement caused by the springs when a car hits a bump. Without shocks, your ride would be an endless series of bounces. Shock absorbers absorb the energy generated when a wheel hits a bump and converts that energy to heat. Prior to 1982, F-bodies used a shock absorber at each wheel. From 1982 on, Mac-Pherson struts have been used on the front.

The typical factory shock exerts its dampening force mainly on the rebound stroke. When a wheel hits a bump, the shock offers small resistance. The major portion of the shock's dampening force is exerted when the wheel is on the way back down to the road, and this results in a smoother ride. Most performance shock absorbers divide the dampening closer to a 50:50 ratio which improves handling at the expense of a harder ride. Most of the better shocks today use nitrogen gas to improve shock dampening,

and the gas does provide a mild booster-spring effect. The best shocks, of course, are those that are adjustable. In this way you can fine tune them. Koni shocks have been a favorite because of their high quality and adjustability, which includes adjustability on the front MacPherson struts. They are expensive, though. Other well-known brands include KYB and Monroe.

Stabilizer Bars

If your Camaro or Firebird doesn't have a rear stabilizer bar, adding one will improve its handling more than any other single modification you can make. Even if you've installed larger tires and better shocks, you need a rear bar. Stabilizer bars are designed to twist when a car leans during a turn. When both wheels are pushed up, there is no loading on the bar. Any resistance is exerted when one wheel hits a bump, or when the car is leaning in a turn. Thus, a stabilizer bar will firm up the ride but nowhere near as much as stiffer springs. That's why it is recommended to retain stock springs, but use stabilizer bars to improve handling, thereby retaining a decent ride.

Generally speaking, you should not replace your stock front bar (at least initially) with a larger bar because you'll be adding understeer. You are better off installing a rear bar, if you don't already have one.

The addition of a rear bar will do wonders. Dollar for dollar, a rear stabilizer bar is by far the most cost-effective suspension modification you can make.

You can also enhance the performance of any bars that are already on the car by substituting polyurethane bushings and end link bushings for the stock rubber ones. Solid polyurethane bushings will make your bar act or have the same effect as a 20–25 percent larger bar. Also, bar response time will be quicker as there is no wait for the rubber bushings to compress before they take effect.

Another point worth considering when selecting a bar is the material it is made from. Some aftermarket suppliers use a better than stock 5150H or 6150H spring steel. Avoid bars made from 1018 cold-roll mild steel. This material is easier and cheaper to manufacture, but lacks the necessary spring qualities needed in a stabilizer bar. Also avoid bars with welded ends.

You can use the following chart to show you the difference or increase in torsional stiffness as bar size increases:

Low-pressure-gas Koni shocks and struts are an excellent way to improve handling on the F-body. They can be tuned for a particular driving style or use because they are adjustable. Koni

Torsional Stiffness Chart

| Front Bar | | Rear Bar | |
Size (in)	Stiffness Increase (%)	Size (in)	Stiffness Increase (%)
5/8	100	1/2	100
3/4	160	5/8	167
7/8	200	11/16	179
15/16	210	3/4	212
1	226	7/8	222

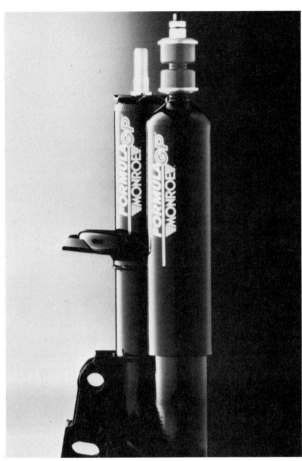

There are many brands of aftermarket shocks and struts to choose from. Shown are offerings from Monroe and KYB. The Monroe shock comes with polyurethane bushings.

Polyurethane antisway bar and end link bushings are an inexpensive way to increase antisway bar performance. They also decrease the bar's reaction time before they take effect. Global West Suspension Components

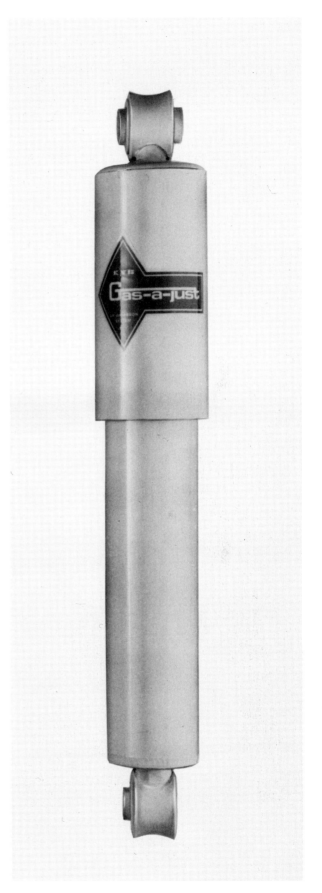

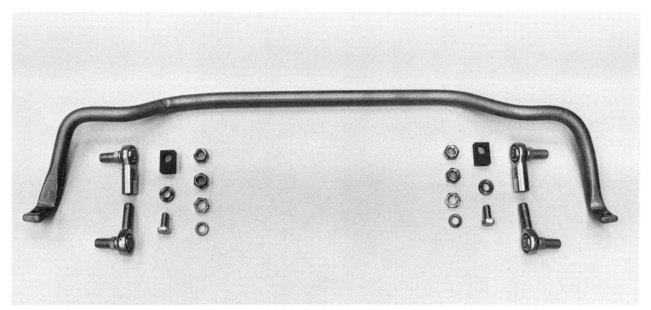

A competition antisway bar like this will usually have adjustable end links, enabling the bar to be tuned for a particular track or application. Herb Adams

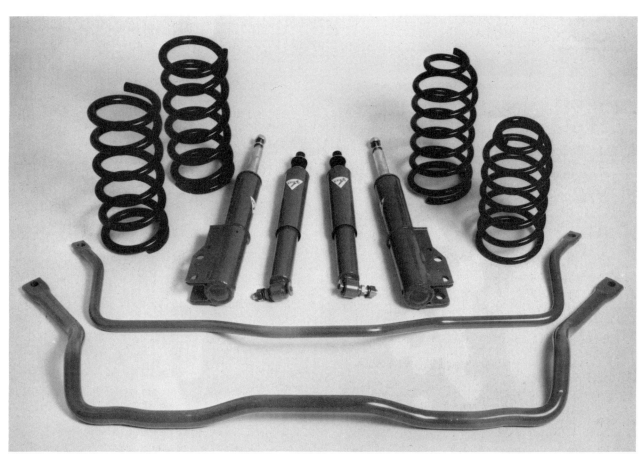

To completely transform a non-Z-28 or Trans Am/Formula suspension you'll need to use a kit that includes shocks, struts, antisway bars, and new springs. Koni

Over the past ten years, the stock front bar size has ranged from 1.06 to 1.40in (27 to 36mm), with the larger 1.40in bar being hollow. You can upgrade your stock bar to one of these. From the aftermarket, about the largest front bar currently available is the one from Addco Industries, Incorporated, which measures 1½in (38.5mm). They recommend using this bar on the street along with a ¾in (29mm) rear bar as these bars won't sacrifice ride quality. For competition use, Addco recommends going to a smaller front bar measuring 1¼in (32mm) in conjunction with a larger ⅞in (22mm) bar. High-performance Trans Ams and Camaros have come with rear bars

measuring 0.82–0.98in (21–25mm), while base models with upgraded factory suspension options (such as the F41) have come with smaller rear bars in the 0.70in (18mm) range.

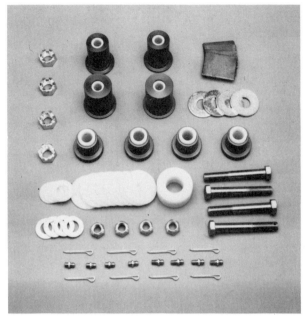

To make sure the suspension stays within set alignment values during hard cornering, acceleration, and braking, you'll need to replace the stock rubber control arm bushings with something harder, such as the Del-A-Lum bushings from Global West. Global West Suspension Components

This is a heavy-duty rear control arm kit for 1982–92 F-bodies. Bushings are much firmer than the stock ones, translating to better traction and handling. Global West Suspension Components*

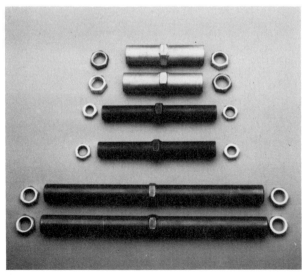

Heavy-duty tie rod sleeves should be used to replace the stock stamped sleeves which can flex under the severe loads imposed by high-performance tires. Global West Suspension Components

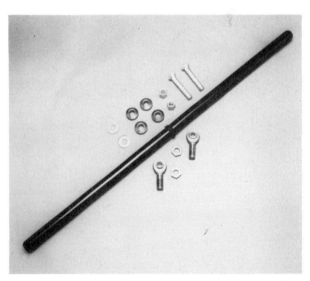

Once you start, there is no stopping in what you can do to improve your car's handling. Keeping the rear axle in place under hard cornering will require that you replace the stock rubber bushed track bar with a Panhard rod that won't deflect. Global West Suspension Components

As can be seen, the stock antisway bar sizes on the performance F-bodies from 1985 are fairly large already and the differences that you find have been attempts by the factory to fine tune the suspension from year to year rather than to gain large incremental improvement. The stock bars are definitely in the ball park—the car is at the stage now where better handling will either be at the expense of ride deterioration (as is autocross and slalom modifications) or through wider and stickier tires.

For the front end, this steering brace will help reduce frame flex at the steering box location. The result is improved responsiveness. Global West Suspension Components

Other Modifications

Other ways to improve handling include moving the battery to the trunk, which improves weight distribution by about 1 percent. The F-body cars are front heavy, so any modification that reduces front end weight, such as a fiberglass hood, will improve handling. Aerodynamic aids, wings spoilers, and side skirts will improve your car's appearance, but their benefits are effective only at very high speeds.

Once you get beyond stabilizer bars, shocks, and springs you'll find that the F-body platform is not as stiff as it could be. You can feel the body flex under hard cornering, especially on the convertibles, which are already loose. As a car's cornering capability is improved, the loads transmitted to the chassis via the suspension attachment points are also correspondingly higher. If these attachment points aren't strengthened, the car's chassis will flex, which has a negative effect on handling. In time, cracks will develop at the suspension attachment points and on the suspension members as well. This can also be compounded by installing springs that are too firm for street use.

Subframe connectors, strut and shock tower braces, rocker stiffeners, and other chassis stiffening components are available from various sources. Other modifications, such as relocating suspension components, aren't recommended or needed for street use. They require a high degree of skill and knowledge and are designed to provide superior handling on the racetrack. It is best to leave the suspension in its stock configuration.

What good handling is all about—this Firebird goes where it is pointed. A car that handles well and predictably *enables the driver to easily set it up for the next turn.* Dennis Ashlock/Firestone

However, for the racer there are some nifty suspension pieces available. Art Morrison Enterprises Incorporated has a front end conversion kit that allows for a 4in ride height adjustment. The kit uses a chrome-moly lower tubular control arm, special coil springs, and adjustable mounts. Because the lower control arm is lighter, you can expect a 40lb weight reduction from the front suspension. Bell Tech has special front spindles that allow for a 2in reduction in front ride height while allowing for correct suspension geometry. As stated earlier, though, lowering your Camaro or Firebird for street use is not recommended.

If you have a 1982–83 F-body car, you may want to consider changing power steering boxes. These cars used a Model 605 power steering box whereas later cars used a Model 800 box which can easily be identified by its use of four bolts holding the rectangular side cover on. The 605s used a round side cover held in place by a retaining ring. The 800 box is better because of its 14:1 overall ratio and better feel. You can use an 800 box if you also replace the pitman arm to an 800 box arm, part number 7837642. The best 800 boxes are from high-performance F-bodies such as the Z-28, IROC, GTA, and Trans Am but because of different size wheel and tire combinations used over the years, you'll find that some boxes have more or less travel built-in in order to prevent the tires from hitting the fenders and suspension. This is accomplished by differing the thickness of internal stops (see chart).

One final point to consider is alignment. Alignment angles of the front suspension influence a car's steering ease, steering stability, ride quality, and tire wear. This is a complex subject because these angles vary as the suspension does its job and the body moves up and down in relation to the wheels. The load in a car and its speed may also cause these angles to change. In addition, they are affected by changes in the car's attitude caused by acceleration, braking, and the type of road surface and cornering forces.

Camber is the amount (measured in degrees) that the front wheels tilt in or out at the top when viewed from the front of the car. When the top of the wheel leans inward, camber is negative. It is best to try for zero camber when aligning the front wheels. A little negative camber will help cornering, from zero to 1/2deg, but any more than this will cause uneven tire wear. With zero camber, the full width of the tire's tread makes contact with the road.

Caster refers to the angle made by a line between the upper and lower steering pivots (ball joints) and a vertical reference line. The angle is positive when this line tilts backward (when the upper ball joint is behind the lower ball joint). It is negative when the line tilts forward (when the upper ball joint is in front of the lower). Positive caster is beneficial as it keeps the wheels pointed straight ahead and reduces any tendency for the car to wander at high speeds. Caster also causes the steering wheel to return to the straight-ahead position as you exit a turn.

Toe is the difference (distance) between the front and rear inside edges of the front tires. Toe is usually set "in," measured in inches. Toe-in increases high-speed stability and takes the slack out of the suspension as the car moves from rest. Incorrect toe greatly affects tire wear.

In SCCA's all-out Trans-Am series, you'll find that the cars barely lean at all through the corners. The suspension is set up to take advantage of wide, low-profile tires, with little regard for values necessary in a street car, such as ride quality, tread wear, and the like. Mark Weber/ Firestone

If you own a Z-28 or Trans Am, consider yourself lucky. You already own one of the best handling production cars built in the United States. You can fine tune the suspension to improve handling as shown here, but your best bet is to improve your driving skills to take advantage of what you already have. You'd be amazed what your car can do in the right hands!

Model 800 Steering Gears

Application	GM Service #	Hollander #	ID Code	Travel
1982 and up F-body, 15in wheels	7839897	1271	WS	35 degrees
1985 and up F-body, 16in wheels (includes FE2)	7843512	1331	HX	32 degrees
1984 and up G-Body w/performance suspension	7843135	1282	YA	39 degrees 15 minutes

Chart courtesy Lee Power Steering. ID codes can be found on the steering box cover and end cap.

Alignment Recommendations

	Caster (deg)		Camber (deg)		Toe Total (in)
	L	**R**	**L**	**R**	
Street	+4	+4½	−½	−½	³/₃₂
Hard Street Use	+5	+5½	−1	−1	³/₃₂
Road Racing	+6	+6	−1¾	−1¾	Short course ⅛ out Long course ¹/₁₆ in
Drag Racing	+4	+4	0	0	¹/₃₂

Note: These settings are a suggested starting point. Measurements were taken with driver weight included. Courtesy of Global West Suspension Components.

The 1993 F-body uses a traditional front engine/rear wheel drive configuration. A major difference from third-generation cars is the use of a short/long arm front suspension. The rear suspension is basically unchanged from the 1992 cars. Chevrolet Motor Div.

Chapter 10

Tires and Wheels

After you find the right mechanical combination for your car and driving style, you are still left with the greatest handling variable: tires. Over the past twenty years we've seen some progress with suspension components—larger antisway bars, new bushing materials, rear disc brake, and the like—yet it's tire engineering and technology that has changed by leaps and bounds. Aspect ratios, construction type, tread designs—in fact, every facet of tire engineering is constantly evolving in the search for the ultimate tire, the tire that will perform well under every possible driving condition and last practically forever. Unfortunately, no one tire can do it all. One brand may provide superior dry performance but may not fare so well in wet. Conversely, another tire may provide excellent braking response yet when compared to another, may not provide adequate acceleration traction. We're confronted with the old bugaboo—compromise. Everything automotive is a compromise, and it extends to tires as well.

If you've ever talked to anyone who races in autocrosses, you'll find that when talk shifts to what modifications they've made or what the trick setup is, the subject most talked about is tires. Tires are the key. For example, in SCCA's stock classes where no deviations from stock are allowed except for tires, a lousy driver driving a car with great tires can beat a

VEHICLE TOP SPEED MPH	INFLATION PRESSURE INCREASE[1] PSI	LOAD CAPACITY[2] (% of maximum branded load on tire)
100	0	100
106	1.5	100
112	3.0	100
118	4.5	100
124	6.0	100
130	7.5	100
137	7.5	90
143	7.5	85
149	7.5	80
155	7.5	75
161	7.5	70
168	7.5	65
174	7.5	60
180	7.5	55
186	7.5	50

1-Do not exceed the maximum pressure branded on tire sidewall.
2-Tire upsizing may be necessary to achieve these reduced loads.

The faster you go, the more air pressure you'll need to put in your tires, according to the European Tyre and Rim Technical Organization Manual. *As indicated by the chart, for speeds up to 100mph, standard inflation pressure applies.*

The majority of F-body cars have been equipped with 14in rims with a 70 or a 75 series tire. A tall tire such as this one reduces cornering limits, and the whitewall also gives a nonperformance look.

good driver with stock tires. Tires make all the difference, and whatever class you look at, the situation is the same. Of course, the tires used in a typical autocross event shouldn't be used on the street because they are made from very soft compounds and tread life is very poor. Two to three weeks of street use is all they're good for.

What is a performance tire? Simply put, a performance tire will respond to steering input with less lag than a non- or low-performance tire. It will be able to corner at higher speeds in a predictably tight manner, and it will have a noticeable on-center feel. Usually such a tire will have a wider tread and a smaller aspect ratio. One thing that *doesn't* make a performance tire, though, is raised white letters.

The advantage of a wider tread is obvious: Increase the tire's contact patch with the road and you should have better traction. The ultimate, in this case, is the racing slick. Unfortunately, in the real world you may occasionally have to deal with rain. A tread pattern, necessary to remove water so that the tire won't hydroplane, also removes some of the tire's contact patch. The tire designer has to compromise, making the tire safe in the wet, while minimizing dry traction loss. We'll look into aspect ratios a little later on.

Construction Types

Original equipment tires in the 1960s were of the bias or the bias belted types. In both of these types the cords that make the tire's plies run crisscross over the tread, from bead to bead. This sort of construction, while quite strong, causes the sidewalls to be very stiff. Thus, for example, in a hard corner there is a tendency for the tread to lift because the sidewall is so stiff. Other disadvantages include tread squirm, which causes wear and heat build-up, and bias-type tires will expand in size the faster you go.

With the bias belted tire, such as Goodyear's old Polyglas GT, two additional belt plies were added

The 15x7in aluminum wheels have been standard equipment on the Z-28 and, starting in 1990, standard on all Camaros. In the 1960s and 1970s, a 15x7in wheel was considered high performance, but today it is merely the starting point.

The 1985 IROC Camaros were the first to come with 16in wheels and 50 series rubber—one of the reasons why it handled so well.

The 1990–92 Z-28s are equipped with 16x8in aluminum wheels fitted with P245/50ZR16 Goodyear Eagle GAs. The trend is toward even taller 17 and even 18in wheels to accommodate the use of increasingly lower profile tires on the street.

between the bias plies and tread. These served to strengthen the tread area, but at best, the bias belted tires were a stopgap measure until the tire manufacturers tooled up for radials.

The main difference between the bias types and radial tires is that the radials' plies run directly across the tread. While strong, these radial plies are very flexible and require the use of belt plies under the tread to provide stiffness. You can visualize a radial tire by looking at an inner tube. By itself, it is wobbly and wouldn't be of much use as a tire. Wrapping a steel belt tightly around its circumference provides a contact patch that will not distort, and because the sidewall is flexible, much more of the tire's tread remains on the ground during hard cornering. The radial's belts also restrict tire expansion as the tire rolls faster and faster. Ever see a fuel dragster burnout? The slicks, which are of a bias-type construction, expand tremendously under acceleration. This won't happen with a radial design.

Other radial tire advantages include less rolling resistance and better wear characteristics.

Aspect Ratio

Aspect ratio is a measure of the tire's height versus its width. Thus a 60 series tire has section height that is 60 percent of its width. A shorter sidewall (a lower aspect ratio) means that the tire will respond quicker to steering input. When you turn your car's steering wheel, the tire doesn't immediately follow. First, the sidewalls bend and the force they exert will eventually overcome the tread's grip on the road and soon the car will turn. A shorter sidewall is stiffer, thus forcing the tread to react quicker. The difference between the direction the tire is pointing and the direction it is steered is called the slip angle. Thus in any cornering situation, you have to steer further into the direction you want to go than the tire will actually go. However, a performance tire will generate a much smaller slip angle, thereby requiring less steering angle for a given corner.

Why have slip angles at all, then? Without slip angles, your car would not turn, no matter how hard you turned the steering wheel, because the tires would just slide. And as mentioned in the case with bias ply tires, very stiff sidewalls have a tendency to lift the tread off the ground during hard cornering. The tire engineer has to balance a host of factors in order to maintain the correct amount of sidewall flexibility for a particular application.

The Goodyear Eagle is a unidirectional tire, meaning it has to be installed with the tread pattern pointing toward the front of the car. The unidirectional tires' only shortcoming is that they aren't that great in the wet. A good alternative for a street car is the Eagle GT4—an all-weather design. Goodyear Tire & Rubber Co.

The Goodyear Eagle ZR35 is a high-performance tire based on the original Eagle GT design. It is a Z-rated tire, good to speeds of 149mph and higher. This one is 315mm wide and requires a 17in rim. Goodyear Tire & Rubber Co.

Also, the slip angle and load exerted on a tire are related. When a tire is loaded it will generate cornering force at a lower slip angle. In a corner, weight distribution is shifted, thereby loading one tire more than the other, even though they both may have the same slip angles. This means they are not generating the same amount of cornering power. The factory engineer's efforts to control weight transfer may be limited by such considerations as a particular type of ride dictated by corporate policy but the enthusiast, through the correct use of springs, shocks, and antisway bars can further minimize it.

It is unlikely that you'll go to your local tire dealer and get into an involved discussion about slip angles with the salesperson. You have to rely on tests you have read about, the tire maker's advertising, your own experience, and any word-of-mouth information you may have acquired to make a sensible choice. However, as a general rule, a tire with a smaller aspect ratio will make smaller slip angles. Installing a 50 or 60 series radial tire on your car will provide better handling. You won't be at the cutting edge of tire technology as the current hot-shot street tires require 17in rims to compensate for a 35 series aspect ratio, but you'll be way ahead of anything that came as standard equipment on the base and six-cylinder models. Going beyond a 50 series tire with stock rims, however, will drastically decrease ground clearance.

The Hi-Tech Turbo style wheel that is most often seen on the Trans Am. If you decide to install aftermarket wheels, try to hold on to them because the third-generation Trans Am will eventually become a collectible. Resist the temptation to dump them.

Tires like this one which are used on cars that autocross should never be used on the street. The rubber compound, with a typical tread wear rating of 50, is far too soft for street use. Tire pressure is upped to 42lb in front, while it is lowered to 24lb in the rear on this IROC-Z. More than anything else, it is the tire that makes all the difference in such an application, all other things being equal.

Firestone has recently entered the high-performance tire arena. This is their Firehawk SV. Firestone

Tire Sizing

As a general rule, you should be able to go one size larger than whatever size came as stock. Typical F-body wheelwells have plenty of space so you can go pretty wild, if you want to. It all depends on how you are using your car.

Tire size designations have changed several times in the last twenty years. Until 1968, US manufacturers used the Numeric System. For example, a tire with 7.00x14 designation meant that the tire had a cross-section width (not tread width) of about 7in when inflated. The 00 part of the number stood for aspect ratio, generally an industry standard of 92, and the 14 stood for rim diameter. A tire with numbers other than 00 usually had a lower profile, which in most cases was around 80.

In 1968, the Alpha Numeric System was adopted. In this system, tires were designated by their load carrying capacity (letters A through N) and their aspect ratio. Thus with an F70x14 tire the F indicates its load capacity, the 70 its aspect ratio, and the 14 its rim width. If the tire was a radial, the letter R would be sandwiched between the F and 70 (FR70x14).

From 1976 on, the P metric system came into use. It gave us more information. For example, a P205/70R-14 would break down as follows: The P stands for passenger tire, the 205 measures its section width in millimeters, 70 stands for aspect ratio, R is for a radial type (B for bias belted, D for bias), and 14 for rim width, still measured in inches. A speed-rated tire will include additional information. The speed rating, expressed by a letter, indicates the tire's ability to withstand high speed and is placed before the letter showing what kind of tire it is. In our example, an H-rated tire would now read as P205/70HR-14. The following are the Speed Symbols currently in use:

Speed Symbol	Maximum Speed (mph)
Q	99
R	106
S	112
T	118
U	124
H	130
V (without Service Description)	130 and above
V (with Service Description)	149
Z	149 and above

Some high-performance speed-rated tires may carry additional information known as the Service Description. This consists of the Load Index (which ranges from 75 [851lb] to 100 [1,760lb] and the Speed Symbol. The Load Index is the same as the load capacity which is normally embossed on the tire's sidewall. Thus, in our example, a P205/70R14 93H tire has a 93 Load Index and is H speed rated. By 1991, all speed-rated tires up to and including H-rated use a Service Description. V-rated tires are marked in three different ways. For example, a P205/70VR-14 tire is certified for speeds above 130mph. A P205/70R14 93V has a Service Description designator and thus is rated for speeds up to 149mph. Finally, with a P205/70VR14 93V, the V speed indicator appears in both size and Service Description, which means that the tire is good to 149mph. Z-rated tires will continue to be identified with the Speed Symbol in the size designa-

Wheels do make the car. This is a variety of aftermarket wheels. You won't see many cars with real modular wheels on the street because of their high cost. However, you will see many wheels emulating the modular look by using simulated rivets.

tion. Pretty complicated, you say? It will probably get even more complicated in the future.

For high-speed driving, additional inflation pressure and possibly reduced tire loading or upsizing is required. You can use the guidelines set in the *European Tyre and Rim Technical Organization Standards Manual* (see chart). What it means is that the faster you go, the more you have to increase inflation pressure, but you aren't supposed to exceed the maximum on the tire's sidewall. And as you go faster, the tire's load capacity is also reduced so you may have to go to a higher load tire.

The drag racer look isn't the best way to go for a street car. The large rear slicks are best for straight-line acceleration, but the skinny front tires are lethal when it comes to braking and cornering.

DOT Designations

Additional designations are required by the Department of Transportation (DOT). They are Tread Wear, Traction, and Temperature gradations which are to help the typical consumer compare one tire with another.

Tread Wear is a comparative index that measures wear rate. A tire rated 200 will wear twice as long as one rated 100. This means that a tire with a low wear rating number will have tread made of a softer rubber and thus provide better traction. I feel that anything in the 300 range and above will give good wear but because the rubber compound is so hard, may provide less than satisfactory traction, especially in the wet. For good handling, you should try and stay under the 200 range. If you are concerned about tread wear, try to modify your driving habits.

The greatest effect on tire wear is caused by braking. A tire will wear four times as fast in a typical moderate stop from 30mph than from a tire that just rolls to a stop. A panic stop that doesn't lock the brakes will cause the tire to wear 2,000–3,000 times faster! Hard cornering will also accelerate wear. Doubling the corner speed of any curve that you take will increase tire wear by sixteen times. Of course, burnout starts and panic stops really shorten tire life. In addition, the higher the temperature outside, the greater the wear. Thus a tire will wear faster, some 20 percent faster, if the outside temperature increases from 45 to about 70 degrees Fahrenheit. Conversely, tread wear is reduced when outside temperature drops from 90 to 50 degrees.

Traction is graded A, B, or C. This gradation measures the tire's ability to stop in the wet. There is no

On the racetrack is where you'll see tire technology take great strides. Wider and lower profile tires along with specific tire compounds matched to racing conditions are the norm. Advances made on the track eventually filter down to street tires. Chevrolet Motor Division

reason to buy anything less than an A-rated tire. *Temperature* is also graded A, B, or C. This measures the tire's ability to withstand and dissipate heat. Again, an A rating is the only way to go, especially if you are going to drive fast, even for a short spurt.

What about rotation? Rotating your tires regularly is very important for long tire life. Regardless of what you may have heard, it is now OK to cross-rotate radial tires. For rear-wheel-drive cars, the right rear tire goes to the right front position, the right front tire moves to the left rear, the left rear to the left front, and the left front to the right rear. You should rotate your tires every 7,500 miles.

The biggest wheel and tire combination during 1982–84 on the Z-28 and Trans Am was 15x7in wheels with P215/65R15 Goodyear Eagle GTs. Four- and six-cylinder-equipped cars have come with 14x6 and 14x7in rims. In 1984, on the Fifteenth Anniversary Edition Trans Am, Pontiac went to 16x8in rims with 50 series Goodyear Eagle GTs measuring P245/50R16. In 1985, the IROC-optioned Camaro got the same size tires while an optional 60 series, P235/60VR15 was available on 15in wheel equipped cars. To date, the largest wheel and tire combination on either Camaro or Trans Am has remained at 16x8in, with the top optioned tires carrying a Z rating.

Your best bet for improved handling is to buy the largest wheel and tire combination that will fit your car and budget. Stick to well-known tire brands. You can upgrade to the factory sizes which between 1982 and 1992 are 15x7 or 16x8in wheels with 65, 60, 55, or 50 series tires. You can't go wrong using a factory combination, but from there on, it all depends on your budget. As long as you maintain a 24–25in overall tire diameter, you can even go to a 17in wheel. The 1992 SLP Firehawk comes with 17x9.5in front and rear wheels fitted with Firestone SZ P275ZR40x17 tires.

Backspacing, or the distance from the wheel's mounting surface to the rim flange, is vital when choosing an aftermarket wheel. If you buy wheels through the mail, make sure to measure the backspacing of your original wheels and the total distance from the mounting surface to any suspension member.

RPM SHOWN AT 60 MPH

REAR END RATIO	TIRE DIAMETER 24"	26"	28"	30"	32"	34"	36"	38"	40"	42"
2.18	1831	1690	1570	1465	1373	1293	1221	1157	1099	1046
2.50	2100	1938	1800	1680	1575	1482	1400	1326	1260	1200
2.74	2301	2124	1973	1841	1726	1625	1534	1454	1381	1315
3.08	2587	2388	2218	2070	1940	1826	1725	1634	1552	1478
3.23	2713	2504	2326	2170	2035	1915	1809	1714	1628	1550
3.50	2940	2714	2520	2352	2205	2075	1960	1857	1764	1680
3.73	3133	2892	2686	2507	2349	2212	2089	1979	1880	1790
3.90	3276	3024	2808	2621	2457	2312	2184	2069	1966	1872
4.10	3444	3179	2952	2755	2583	2431	2296	2175	2066	1968
4.56	3830	3536	3283	3064	2873	2704	2554	2419	2298	2189
4.88	4099	3784	3513	3279	3074	2894	2733	2589	2460	2342

$$\text{FORMULA}: \frac{\text{MPH} \times \text{AXLE RATIO} \times 336}{\text{TIRE DIAMETER}}$$

This chart will help you choose a tire that is compatible with the rear axle ratio on your car. The lower the rpm at 60mph, the better mileage you'll get, plus longer engine life. Crane Cams, Inc.

If it is time to replace your Goodyear Eagles, consider replacing your worn-out tires with the Eagle GT+4s. Somewhat less expensive yet still providing excellent all-weather performance are Firestone's Firehawk, BFGoodrich's Comp T/A HR, and General Tire's XP2000 AS.

The Formula Firehawk is equipped with Firestone Firehawk SZ 40 series tires measuring P275/40ZR17. Seventeen-inch rims are required to maintain stock ride height. Taller rims with lower profile tires are becoming the norm, and you can expect even taller rims in the future. SLP Engineering, Inc.

Naturally, when you are replacing tires, get tires that are rated at least HR (good to 130mph) or VR (good over 130mph).

Wheels

Standard F-body wheels have measured 14x6 or 14x7in. These are of the pressed-steel variety with optional 15x7 and 16x8in wheels made of aluminum.

Most aftermarket replacement wheels are made of aluminum as are the optional stock wheels. Aluminum wheels are stronger than the stock stamped-steel wheels which can deflect under hard cornering, and aluminum wheels also contribute to reduced unsprung weight. Unsprung weight consists of weight that is not supported by the car's springs, such as wheels, tires, brakes, and hubs. A lighter wheel contributes to less overall weight and less unsprung weight which can be felt as reduced shock to the car's springs when going over bumps.

The majority of aftermarket wheels are made from aluminum or an aluminum alloy, and can either be cast or forged. Forged wheels are more expensive, but they are stronger. There are also two- and three-piece modular wheels to choose from. By using different sections, wheel width and offset can be changed to accommodate different tires for different applications, thereby offering a distinct advantage to the racer.

Both the 1993 Camaro and Z-28 are equipped with 16in wheels. At 8in, the Z-28's are ½in wider, and they are made of aluminum. The standard tire on the Z-28 is the Goodyear Eagle GA P235/55R16. Optional is the Goodyear P245/50ZR16 Eagle GS-C. Chevrolet Motor Div.

Most enthusiasts have heard of positive and negative offset as well as wheel backspacing. A negative offset wheel is said to have the tire's centerline outboard of the wheel's centerline—this is typical of the deep-dish look. The opposite occurs with positive offset, which is found on most front-wheel-drive cars.

Backspacing is the distance from the wheel's mounting surface to the back rim flange. This isn't the same as offset. Two wheels can have the same offset, but the wider of the two wheels will have a larger backspacing. Too much backspacing and the wheels will hit your suspension.

The Plus System

The Plus System is an easy way to figure out the tire and wheel combination to use when going to a wider tire, yet still remaining within safe load carrying capacities and also maintaining the same overall diameter for speedometer accuracy.

For example, a 1985 base Firebird comes with 14x6in wheels fitted with P205/70R14 tires. The next size wider tire is a P215 but in order to maintain the same diameter (the P215/70R14 would be taller), you'd have to go to a lower profile tire on a taller rim, a P215/60R15. In this way you've lowered the tire's aspect ratio while increasing the tire's contact patch. This is referred to as Plus 1 because you've increased wheel diameter by one size and aspect ratio by one size. A Plus 2 would increase diameter and aspect ratio by two sizes. In our example, then, a Plus 2 would be a P225/50R16.

Naturally, when you are using the Plus System, you must refer to the manufacturer's tire availability and load capacity charts in order to match the tires to the right wheels.

Of course, if you are on a tight budget (and who isn't?) and can't afford to get new wheels and tires, you may be better off getting the widest low-profile tires that will safely fit on your wheels and just change the speedometer gear to compensate for the different height.

Figuring Out Effective Axle Ratio

The bigger a tire's diameter, the less acceleration you'll have, while a tire that's smaller than stock will improve acceleration. The following formula will make it easy for you to find out what your effective axle ratio will be after changing from a stock tire (for example, P205/70R14) to a taller tire such as a P255/60VR15.

$$\frac{\text{New tire revs/mile}}{\text{Original tire revs/mile}} \text{ x Original axle ratio} = \text{Effective axle ratio}$$

$$\frac{773}{825} \text{ x } 3.08 = 2.88$$

Thus in this example, installing taller tires will reduce your effective axle ratio from to 3.08:1 to 2.88:1. This will result in better mileage at the expense of acceleration. To regain equivalent acceleration, the rear axle must be changed. The following formula will tell you what axle ratio you will need.

$$\frac{\text{Original tire revs/mile}}{\text{New tire revs/mile}} \text{ x Original axle ratio} = \text{Equivalent axle ratio}$$

$$\frac{825}{773} \text{ x } 3.08 = 3.28$$

So in order to duplicate stock acceleration, a 3.28:1 axle ratio is needed. The closest one available is a 3.23:1, which is close enough.

Chapter 11

Brakes

In keeping with a performance-minded attitude, most of the emphasis in this book is on making your Camaro and Firebird go faster and handle better. In doing so, you could easily forget about your brakes. The faster your car goes the more stopping power it needs. Stock brakes are adequate for everyday use but the minute you start using your brakes harder than normal, you'll soon notice that the brakes will "fade."

What is happening is that your brakes take the forward motion (kinetic energy) of your car and convert it into another form of energy, in this case, heat. When brakes fade, it means that they cannot continue converting the car's forward motion into heat because they are too hot and need some time to cool and dissipate the heat.

You can tell when your brakes are fading when it takes more and more brake pedal travel to stop or slow down the car, and sometimes even pushing the pedal to the floor won't stop the car. This is often accompanied by increased pedal effort—you have to press the brake pedal harder and harder. And you can smell what is happening as the brake pads and shoes heat up and start to smoke.

The problem with heat buildup is that it can damage your brakes beyond repair. The discs and drums may be scored or warped and under severe use, the disc pads and drum shoes can also disinte-

All 1982 and later Camaros and Firebirds came with power front disc brakes measuring 10.5in except on those equipped with the 1LE option which measured 11.9in. An advantage of disc brakes is their greater swept (braking) area per given size and the rotor is always exposed to air and thus cools faster. Maintenance is also easier as pads can be quickly changed.

On the rear you'll find finned drum brakes. Rear disc brakes have been optional since 1982, measuring 10.5 or 11.7in depending on the customer's preference. Rear discs have considerably more resistance to fade, but even with discs, the stock setup could be improved with an adjustable proportioning valve. In stock form, the rear brakes lock up prematurely.

This is Wilwood's Super Stopper front disc brake kit, which features 12in vented rotors, billet aluminum hubs, and massive four-piston aluminum calipers. The kit comes complete with new front bearings and hardware and is designed for 1982 and later F-bodies that originally came with 10.5in rotors. Wilwood Engineering

Wilwood's 12in front assembly (the rear disc uses the same rotor). The caliper features quick-change brake pads. This unit is suitable for light road-racing use. Wilwood Engineering

grate. If you are going to use your brakes hard, there are certain things you can do to reduce fade and improve your Camaro's or Firebird's braking performance.

All F-bodies built since 1982 come with power front disc brakes and rear drum brakes as standard equipment; these work fine under normal use. The front disc brakes do most of the work—usually two-thirds of the braking action is handled by the front brakes. The automobile industry gradually switched over to front disc brakes by the mid-1970s because disc brakes are more resistant to brake fade, provide greater braking power over a comparable drum brake, and are much easier to service and maintain. The main reason disc brakes are better than drum brakes is that the braking surface is directly exposed to air so that cooling begins immediately. In a drum brake, the heat generated by braking action is inside the drum and it takes time for this heat energy to dissipate.

The standard brakes on Camaros and Firebirds since 1982 have been 10.5in disc brakes up front, with 9.5in drum brakes in the rear. An optional four-wheel disc brake setup that substitutes 10.5in rear disc brakes for the drums has also been available. Up to 1989, the calipers used on these brakes were iron but have been replaced with aluminum units since then.

The aluminum calipers have considerably more corrosion resistance than the iron units.

1993 Camaros and Firebirds are equipped with power front discs and rear drums that measure 10.9in in front and 9.5in in the rear. The Z-28 and Trans Am come with a standard four-wheel disc system that uses 10.9in front and 11.4in rear discs. Both use GM's ABS-VI anti-lock brake system as standard equipment.

For improved braking, there are several paths you can follow, but then again, this all depends on what you're planning to use the car for. If you own a car that has rear drum brakes, you can improve braking performance by replacing the stock brake pads and shoes (more on that later) and by installing an adjustable proportioning valve in the system. One of the deficiencies of all-stock F-body brakes (including those equipped with four-wheel discs) is poor front-to-rear balance. The tendency is for the rear brakes to lock up prematurely under hard braking. With an adjustable proportioning valve you can, with a little experimentation, arrive at a much better front-to-rear balance.

Installing factory rear disc brakes won't necessarily improve overall braking performance, but it will give you more fade resistance on the rear brakes under hard use. Since quite a few F-bodies were built with optional rear discs since 1982, there is a good possibility that you may be able to locate a serviceable rear axle with discs at a salvage yard. In fact, if you want the factory 10.5 or 11.7in (on 350ci equipped cars) discs for the rear, you'll have to replace the rear axle anyway because the discs will not fit cars originally equipped with drums. Drum brake cars use an offset three-bolt flange that is welded on the end of the axle housing to which the drum backing plate attaches, whereas disc brake axles use a four-bolt rectangular plate that mates to the caliper mounting bracket. Still, if you have a pre-1989 four-wheel disc brake car, you can install the later aluminum calipers along with the necessary aluminum caliper mounting plate for whichever rear axle your car is equipped with, either the ten-bolt Saginaw rear or the nine-bolt Borg-Warner.

Aftermarket Front and Rear Disc Brake Conversion Kits

The modifications described thus far are adequate for hard street and light autocrossing use. For more serious applications there are disc brake kits available from JFZ Engineered Products, Incorporated, Wilwood Engineering, and SLP. These companies specialize in brake components for race car use. There is also the possibility of installing the factory 1LE option brakes. The 1LE is a limited-production option aimed for road racing. It consists of larger 12in rotors and lightweight aluminum calipers, similar to those used on the Corvette. You'll find the major parts for converting your brakes to 1LE specs listed here, but it is a rather expensive proposition.

For street use, JFZ has its Series V Front Pro Street kits, which are available in two configurations. The kits can either come with vented rotors measuring 10.25x0.810in or for more stopping power, 12.18x0.810in vented rotors, billet aluminum hubs, four-piston aluminum calipers, bearings, and necessary hardware. The rear kit also uses a 12.18in

rotor. The larger rotors are also available in 1.25in thickness.

Wilwood Engineering has their Super Stopper front disc brake kit for late-model F-bodies. It consists of a 10.75in diameter vented 1.25in thick rotor, Superlite II aluminum four-piston caliper, and hardware. The whole setup weighs 15lb less than the stock components, thereby reducing unsprung weight. With 1lb of rotating weight equal to 10lb of static weight, front end weight is reduced some 300lb when the car is in motion, according to Wilwood.

Wilwood's rear disc brake kit features the same size rotor as the front, but also offers an optional mechanical caliper parking brake.

SLP offers a Brembo 13in diameter disc brake kit. These were originally developed for Ferraris and are DOT legal. The Brembo brakes are optional on the SLP's Firehawk, but they are available in kit form as well. The kit contains a new proportioning valve and mounting bracket, but you must also obtain the special 1LE spindles for the front.

Since it is the front brakes that do most of the work, your first step should be to replace the stock front disc brakes, followed by the rears, especially if you are under any budgetary constraints. In all cases, you should also install an adjustable proportioning valve.

Brake Pad and Shoe Types

Some enthusiasts may think that they can improve brake performance by simply switching to pads and shoes using different types of friction materials.

JFZ's front Series V kit also comes complete and uses grooved rotors for better fade resistance. Rotor measures 12.18in. JFZ Engineered Products, Inc.

Always use vented rotors on a street car because the air circulating between the rotor is what keeps temperature down. The four-piston caliper and 12.18in rotor provide massive stopping power. JFZ Engineered Products, Inc.

It would be great if there was a material that would last a long time, could withstand high temperatures, wouldn't damage the rotor or drum, and would also be quiet. Unfortunately, there isn't such a material. Instead there are several types of materials, each designed for specific purposes.

Organic

The most common material used for brake linings is made from organic sources. This includes asbestos, cashew nut shell liquid, rubber chips, aluminum, brass, lead, and curing agents and phenolic resins used to bind them all together. Because of health questions, the use of asbestos has declined appreciably and is replaced by glass and synthetic fibers. These are molded to the required shape and either riveted or bonded (glued) onto a backing plate. For street use either attachment method is acceptable, but bonded linings do not have high temperature resistance so they should not be used in a performance application.

The advantages of organic linings are low cost, low rate of wear, and they quiet performance. Their disadvantages become readily apparent under hard use—they fade and wear quickly as temperatures reach 400 degrees F. and higher.

Metallic

Under hard usage, the organic materials in conventional linings quickly fall apart because they can't stand the high temperatures. Metallic linings, made from a metallic powder in a process called sintering, where the powder is compressed and molded at high temperatures, can withstand the high temperatures encountered in a race application. However, there are some serious drawbacks to metallic linings. When metallic linings are cold, they don't work too well—they need to get hot to work properly.

This is OK on the racetrack, but not on the street. Metallic linings also wear the rotor and drum surface more and they cost more. They should not be used on a street car.

Semi-Metallic

The semi-metallic lining is the best of both worlds. They are comprised of steel fibers bonded with organic resins to give excellent performance to about 1,000 degrees. However, they shouldn't be used in competition application because the steel fibers will melt and fuse on the rotor or drum surface.

For everyday use, a semi-metallic lining is preferrable. If you are going to do some serious autocrossing or road racing, switch to a metallic pad. This isn't hard to do on disc-brake-equipped cars, and the aftermarket disc brakes are designed for even quicker pad removal and installation.

Finally, whenever you change to new pads, make sure that you break them in properly. This process, called "bedding," is done by driving your car and slowly warming up the brakes by making several light to moderate stops followed by several hard stops. The brakes should then be allowed to cool.

The reason for bedding is to avoid glazing the pads or shoes. Glazing occurs when the lining material is first heated up. The organic components in the lining boil away and if the brakes are heated up too quickly, the material will resolidify on the pad or shoe. This hard surface can only be removed by refacing (or replacing) the pad or shoe.

Whenever changing to rear discs or when road racing, a brake proportioning valve is a nice thing to have because you can alter front-to-rear brake balance. This is JFZ's adjustable unit. JFZ Engineered Products, Inc.

Optional on the SLP Firehawk and also available in kit form for other F-body cars are the 13x1.25in Brembo brakes. They use a grooved and drilled rotor, and you must use the factory 1LE front spindle. A bit of overkill for a street car, perhaps. They are best suited for competition use. SLP Engineering, Inc.

Brake Fluids

Without hydraulic fluid, your braking system would not work. The fluid most commonly used today is a polyalkaline glycol ether mixture. Not all the brake fluids that you see in the typical auto parts store are formulated exactly the same, but all must meet DOT standards. Brake fluid should have certain properties—for example, it should not compress, freeze, or boil and it should be compatible with other glycol-based fluids.

The most important criterion that a brake fluid must have is its resistance to boiling at high temperatures. How does brake fluid boil? When the brakes are used hard, they get hot and that heat is transferred to the brake fluid. Like any other fluid that boils, tiny bubbles are formed in the brake lines and because gas bubbles compress, this results in a spongy pedal. Brake fluid boils at 550 degrees F. but depending on how much water has contaminated the system, this boiling point drops. Brake fluid is very hydroscopic and readily absorbs water.

Brake fluid is rated by DOT as follows:

	DOT 3 (deg F.)	DOT 4 (deg F.)	DOT 5 (deg F.)
Dry boiling point	401	446	500
Wet boiling point	284	311	356

The dry boiling point refers to the boiling point that fresh, out-of-the-can brake fluid has. The wet boiling point refers to fluid that has been exposed to moisture under certain conditions that DOT uses for testing purposes. DOT 3 and 4 standards apply to regular fluid; DOT 5 applies only to silicone-based fluid.

Aftermarket calipers are typically a four-piston design mounted solidly on the spindle rather than floating, as the stockers are. Changing pads is simple. JFZ Engineered Products, Inc.

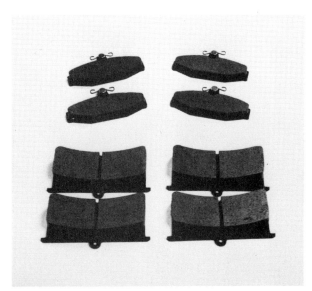

High-performance brake pads and shoes are a must. These are Magnum pads from TPI Specialties. Note that the pads are grooved. For additional brake fade resistance, you can add grooves on the drum shoes (if you have rear drums) and a lengthwise groove on the disc pads. TPI Specialties, Inc.

Tilton's adjustable proportioning valve has seven settings. It can be mounted in any position and the lever may be rotated 360deg. Tilton Engineering Inc.

Tests have shown that the fluid's boiling point in the typical car will decrease by about 100 degrees after six months and by another 25–50 degrees in a year's time. If you plan to do any racing, you should change your fluid every week.

To avoid any future problems with corrosion in your brake system, change the fluid at least every year or 25,000 miles and stick to the same brand. If you change brands, make sure to flush out all the old fluid before replacing it with the new fluid.

Although one may think that you can change the fluid by simply opening up the bleed screws and pumping it out, this won't get all the fluid out because the bleeders are located at high spots—after all, they are designed to let air out, not fluid. You can refill and drain the system several times, each time diluting the fluid, but the only correct way is to disassemble the brake calipers, wheel cylinders, and master cylinder.

You also may have heard of silicone-based brake fluids. Unlike the typical glycol-based fluid, silicone fluids do not absorb moisture so there is no problem with corrosion, and it has a higher boiling point as well. However, it is not recommended for race use because the fluid will compress slightly after exposure to high temperature—resulting in a spongy pedal. For race use, a glycol-based fluid works best, such as JFZ's Z-10 Racing Fluid which has a dry boiling point of 570 degrees.

If you do change to a silicone-based fluid, you must flush out all the existing brake fluid as outlined earlier in order to take advantage of its properties.

Other Modifications

One useful brake system modification would be to install steel braided hoses in place of the stock rubber brake hoses at the wheels. When the brakes are used hard, hydraulic pressure causes the stock rubber hoses to expand, which creates a softer pedal and requires more pumping. This is noticeable in a race application.

On race cars you may have seen rotors that are grooved or drilled with holes. The grooves and holes can reduce fade by letting the gas and dust generated by the brakes go to the grooves or holes instead of forming a lubricating layer between the lining and rotor or drum surface. Grooves are preferable because stress cracks can form around the holes. This modification is not necessary on the street but if you insist on grooving, make grooves on your disc pads and rotors. Some disc pads and shoes already come with grooves—disc pads often come with a single groove and adding another one is acceptable. Brake shoes should have a groove every 2in or so. This no-cost modification will improve fade resistance. Don't overdo it, though, as too many grooves will increase

wear, and always use a respirator mask (like the masks painters use) when cutting the grooves since asbestos is potentially dangerous. Don't get the dust on your hands or clothes, either.

Other modifications and high-performance braking systems are described in Fred Puhn's *Brake Handbook*.

A chart containing major brake component information is located in the appendices of the book you're holding.

1988 and Later GM 1LE Major Brake Components

Group	Description	Part No.	Quantity Needed
4.665	Bracket, front brake caliper mount	18016034	2
4.665	Housing, with piston		
	Front, LH	10132827	1
	Front, RH	10132828	1
	Rear, LH	10132831	1
	Rear, RH	10132832	1
4.665	Plate, anchor		
	Front, LH	10132829	1
	Front, RH	10132830	1
	Rear, LH & RH	10112652	2
4.680	Hose, brake		
	Front, LH	10113075	1
	Front, RH	10113076	1
	Rear, LH (1989–91)	17988596	1
	Rear, RH (1989–91)	17990890	1
5.001	Plate, rear brake caliper mounting		
	Saginaw 10-bolt, LH	10136853	1
	Saginaw 10-bolt, RH	10136854	1
	Borg-Warner 9-bolt, LH	10080875	1
	Borg-Warner 9-bolt, RH	10080876	1
5.017	Pad kit, disc brake		
	Front	10104485	1
	Rear	10174840	1
5.809	Rotor, brake		
	Front	18016035	2
	Rear	10087702	2
6.020	Knuckle, steering		
	LH	18016737	1
	RH	18016738	1

Chapter 12

Bodywork Modifications

Along with the usual mechanical modifications, the typical enthusiast will want his or her Camaro or Firebird to stand out visually as well. This has been common since the late 1960s, when add-ons such as front spoilers, rear wings, and rear window louvers became popular. The front and rear spoilers that originated on the Z-28 Camaro were designed to make the car more aerodynamically stable while rear window louvers, which first appeared on a Corvair show car, are more of a styling add-on.

Spoilers and wings were touted as a way to improve mileage in the 1970s and early 1980s, and they also make the car look more aggressive. With strong engines under the hoods of these cars, it was through bodywork add-ons that the factory used to

convey a performance image, even though their benefits were negligible at typical street speeds.

When the third-generation cars were introduced in 1982, the Z-28 Camaro came with a rear spoiler along with small side and nose skirts. This look has remained essentially unchanged. The Trans Am Firebird came with a similar treatment, but used a rear wing instead of a spoiler. In 1985, the Trans Am came with a more pronounced aero package and an air dam style rear spoiler, although the rear wing spoiler was available on lesser Firebirds.

In 1985, Chevrolet introduced the IROC (International Race of Champions) Camaro which used a more pronounced front spoiler and lower side skirts than the Z-28. There are several kits available to make

The 1991 Camaro Z-28 is still readily identifiable as a third-generation Camaro. Having the same basic body as the original 1982 model, the current Camaro has two lower side scoops and the front and rear lower body *extensions are deeper. The rear spoiler has seen changes over the years as well. How functional this version is over previous designs is not known. Chevrolet Motor Division*

the stock Camaro look like an IROC. The early-1990s Camaro's side panels have been modified slightly to include scoops, and the rear uses a taller spoiler.

Most of the aftermarket kits are designed to give regular Camaros and Firebirds the stock Z-28 or Trans Am aero look, and most of them look similar to one another. One of the best available is the kit from American Best Car Parts Incorporated/Xenon, which is made from polyurethane and guaranteed for life. The polyurethane is stronger and considerably more resistant to cracks than fiberglass.

Besides the kits, the use of a fiberglass hood is also popular. In addition to taking some weight off of the front wheels for better handling, the custom fiberglass hood gives a Camaro or Firebird a high-performance look. A fiberglass hood is also usually necessary with some supercharged applications as well as some aftermarket fuel injection setups because this type of hood allows for taller intake setups.

And of course, if you don't like the stock rear wings or spoilers, there are many aftermarket ones to choose from—and all of them seem to be bigger than the next one.

A 1991–92 Camaro rear spoiler. The lower body extension is deeper on these Camaros than earlier ones. Lower than this might create unnecessary drag at high speeds because it would act as a parachute, trapping air underneath the car and slowing the car down. Late-model Mustang GTs also have this problem.

Plenty of aftermarket add-ons on this Camaro—rear wing, window louvers, and low side skirts are evident. After ten years of having the same basic car produced, it is no wonder that the typical enthusiast would want to give his or her car some distinctiveness.

The vast expanse of the F-body hood lends itself to a variety of aftermarket configurations. Taller hoods are necessary with exotic intake systems but in all cases, because they are made of fiberglass, handling will improve. Anything to reduce weight increases your car's power-to-weight ratio as well. An additional benefit is better engine cooling on designs that have an opening at the rear. The opening lets hot underhood air escape.

A limited run of 1989 Trans Ams came with this rear deck lid, which replaced the stock rear glass hatch. A similar aftermarket fiberglass replica is available from Custom F/X Fiberglass.

Other modifications include tinting the side and rear windows and the use of tinted headlight covers. These should be used with caution, however, as they will decrease visibility at night, and window tinting is not legal in all states. Although you don't see many Camaros or Firebirds so equipped, front end bras are available from many sources. They will protect the front end from bug splatter, but they can also remove your car's paint by the rubbing motion caused by wind if they aren't installed properly.

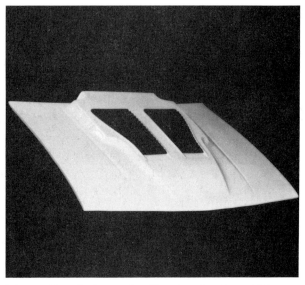

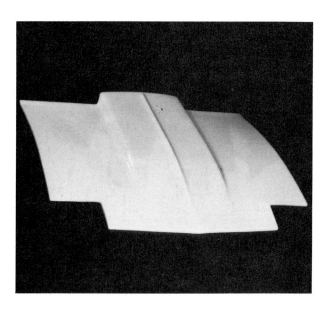

The quality of aftermarket fiberglass hoods and kits can vary. The quality of these hoods from Harwood Industries is excellent. Harwood Industries Inc.

This base Camaro has an IROC Daytona type hood and a front spoiler.

You can update an older Camaro with Kamei's X1 kit. It includes spoilers, air dam, and side treatment. Kamei USA Auto Extras

This is Pacific's aerodynamic styling package for 1985–87 Firebirds. It consists of a front air dam, rocker panel side skirts, door caps, and rear lower wraparound skirt. Pacific Auto Accessories Inc.

For 1990–92 Firebirds, Pacific has this unique urethane kit which consists of a front air dam, door caps, side skirts, and rear lower wraparound skirt while the rear spoiler with integral brake light is made to fit 1982 and later Firebirds. Pacific Auto Accessories Inc.

Neat Top Company offers the Transvertible and Camvertible kits for 1982–91 Firebirds and Camaros. The kit replaces the stock hatchback with an outer fiberglass hatch with a convertible soft top and plastic window that fold up within the fiberglass hatchback. The replacement hatch also has a built-in rear deck spoiler. Neat Top Company

Headlight covers can make the Camaro sleeker looking but also limit light output.

Chapter 13

Interior Modifications

As good as the F-body interior is, there is room for improvement. For example, some owners prefer the feel of leather or wood instead of the vinyl that is used to cover the standard steering wheel. The basic Camaro and Firebird models came with the usual warning lights, but the Z-28s and Trans Ams came with a more informative dashboard. Although the dash comes with oil pressure, temperature, and volt gauges, it would be nice to know what the exact temperature or oil pressure is. The stock gauges show a low, mid, and high numerical setting but many drivers would like to know what the exact oil pressure is, rather than simply knowing it is between 30 and 60lb, for example. The seats have improved over the years but again, they are a compromise designed to fit a variety of driver physiques. There is a lot that can be done here as well.

Instruments

The typical high-performance Camaro or Firebird is equipped with a speedometer and tachometer, and oil pressure, water temperature, fuel, and volt gauges. With these gauges, all the basics are covered. The Camaro and Firebird have shared the same basic interior cabin configuration, but some effort has been made to differentiate between the two dashboards. Camaros have used a large speedometer and tachometer with smaller ancillary gauges located in between the two. Firebirds have used a large four-pod system.

A speedometer measures how fast your car is going, but until mid-1984, Camaros and Firebirds came with an inadequate 85mph speedometer which was well beneath what the typical Z-28 or Trans Am is capable of reaching. In addition, the speedometer was an oddball design, with a single needle indicating speed in both miles per hour and kilometers per hour. From 1985 on, a 140mph speedometer replaced the

Since 1990, Firebird interiors have used a steering-wheel-mounted airbag. The dash configuration uses four round instrument gauges. *This is a 1992 GTA.* Pontiac Motor Division

85mph unit. This was a welcome improvement, even though the higher performance F-bodies are capable of 150mph or close to it. For those wanting a speedometer that reads higher, GM Performance Parts offers a 140mph unit, part number 25052189, that fits 1982–84 cars, but it does have a Z-28 emblem on it. With this speedometer you'll be able to tell how fast you're going, which is especially important on highly modified cars.

The stock tachometer works well enough, but in a race application you'll probably want to install an aftermarket unit that is easier to see when you're driving hard. There are many available from manufacturers such as Stewart-Warner Instrument Corporation, Sun Electric Corp., and Auto Meter Products Incorporated. The most common place you'll find these installed is right on the dash pad. It may not be attractive or integral with the interior, but it gets the job done. Auto Meter's Shift-Lite Sport-Comp Monster tach has an interesting feature—an amber light is activated when a predetermined rpm is reached so the driver doesn't have to look at the tach directly but instead can concentrate on driving. Another Auto Meter tach has a built-in memory function that recalls

The stock Camaro interior dash is basically the same from 1982 to 1992 (1986 shown). It is well thought out and the optional dash on the Z-28 includes gauges that fill the minimum requirements for a performance car—tachometer, oil pressure, water temperature, fuel gauges, and volt meter.

A car with the capabilities of a Z-28 or Trans Am deserves a speedometer that reads at least 10mph higher than its top speed. Early cars came with 85mph speedometers. Late-model cars come with more realistic 140 and 150mph speedometers. This 200mph speedometer and 8000rpm tachometer is designed to fit in the F-body dash. Gale Banks Engineering

Stewart-Warner is a well-known name in automotive instrumentation. They have a variety of gauges that measure every possible automotive function. Stewart-Warner Instrument Corp.

Auto Meter's three-gauge console is designed for under-dash applications. The mechanical gauges measure 2in. Auto Meter Products Inc.

Auto Meter's best competition gauges are liquid filled and are designed to absorb vibrations inherent in a race car. They are large and easy to read. Auto Meter Products Inc.

This is Auto Meter's Sport-Comp Monster tach which has a 5in face and an adjustable shift light. The best place to mount this tach is right on top of the dash. Auto Meter Products Inc.

A recent entry into the auto instruments market is Auto Avionics. These aircraft-quality gauges are offered in a variety of sizes and configurations. Auto Avionics Instrument Research Inc.

This is Grant's Ultimate Wood Touring GT steering wheel. It uses a mahogany wood grip and center cover. It is a great way to add some individuality and class to your Camaro or Firebird interior. Grant Products

the highest rpm reached. These units are also available through GM.

There are three gauges that are considered indispensable in a performance car: oil pressure gauge, water temperature gauge, and an ammeter gauge or volt meter to monitor the car's electrical system. An ammeter gauge shows either a charging or discharging condition in the engine's alternator. A volt meter may indicate the condition of an electrical system more accurately, as it indicates voltage.

If you aren't happy with the stock gauges, there is a slew of aftermarket gauges that you can use. They come in various sizes, but the problem you may have is where to install them. In a race car, the gauges are mounted on a simple piece of sheet metal but on a street car, some kind of fabricated panel is going to be required unless you install one of the available underdash panels. Still, there is plenty of room on the dash.

There is also the question of whether to install mechanical or electrical gauges. Both have their advocates and both are reliable, although you'll find

Another popular Grant wheel is this Touring GT four-spoke model which is available in mahogany, leather, or foam. Steering wheel installation is not difficult, although it does require the use of a steering wheel puller. Grant Products

The Recaro LSC seat, part of their L Modular System. This seat uses the LS back which provides firm support for those desiring a snugger fit. The high sides were designed to keep the driver in place during serious driving. Keiper Recaro Seating, Inc.

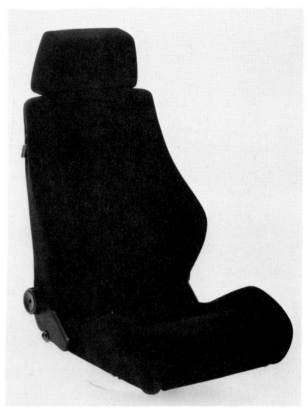

The more affordable Turbo, retaining the features that make a Recaro seat so desirable. The seat has a forward-tilt feature for easier rear seat access. Keiper Recaro Seating, Inc.

134

that most racers use mechanical gauges. A mechanical gauge uses a mechanical method of measuring—for example, a mechanical oil pressure gauge has a small line carrying pressurized oil to it while an electrical gauge uses a sending unit to convert the mechanical movement into an electrical impulse which is then sent to the gauge via a wire. Electrical gauges have the advantage of easier installation.

Besides the three stock gauges mentioned, there are gauges available to measure practically any fluid pressure and temperature found in a car, such as oil temperature, transmission and gear box temperature, turbo boost, manifold pressure, exhaust temperature, brake line pressure, fuel pressure, blower boost, engine vacuum, cylinder head temperature, and air charge temperature. You just have to decide what functions you want to monitor.

Many enthusiasts pooh-pooh warning lights, but in a race situation, you might want to consider installing an additional warning light to indicate low oil pressure. It is difficult to watch the gauges and drive at the same time, and a warning light can grab your attention, especially if you lose oil pressure.

Steering Wheels

When you look at the typical F-body interior, you'll find lots of vinyl- and plastic-covered surfaces—and that includes the steering wheel. The stock steering wheel is small enough and thick enough but if you want to dress up your interior, an easy way is to install an aftermarket steering wheel. Several manufacturers make custom steering wheels, including Grant Products. Grant has a varied line of aftermarket wheels to suit any taste—from solid hardwood and leather to soft foam grips.

The traditional wood steering wheel is a good choice, but there are leather-covered wheels as well. You'll have to stick with the stock steering wheel on cars built after 1990 as these came with an airbag that is housed in the steering wheel. Certain Camaros and Firebirds have also come with various steering-wheel-mounted controls; once again, there's a limit to how much you can do with those steering wheels.

Steering wheel installation is easy. All you'll need is a socket to remove the center wheel shaft nut and you'll probably have to purchase an inexpensive steering wheel puller, if you don't already have one. The whole process shouldn't take more than half an hour.

Hooker's chrome roll bar for street Camaros and Firebirds is a four-point design. It looks great and the rear seats can still be used. Hooker Industries Inc.

*As you'd expect, the 1993 F-bodies got a new interior. This
is the interior of the Z-28. Note the 150mph speedometer.
Chevrolet Motor Div.*

136

Custom Seats

No matter how good you think the stock bucket seats are, you haven't sat in a "good" seat until you've sat in a custom aftermarket seat such as a Recaro. They are designed with a lot more care and because they provide superior support, you'll have a much more comfortable ride and less fatigue over long trips. Custom seats are also designed to fit more snugly than the stock seats, which is important during spirited driving. Proper seating is one of the most overlooked aspects of driving, and it is worth looking into what is available.

Besides providing a more comfortable ride, a racer will want to use the lightest possible seat in order to reduce vehicle weight. There are seats available for this purpose but for a street car, you'll probably want something that is more comfortable and adjustable. Many race seats are made to fit only one driver and are bolted down in that driver's preferred position.

The typical stock seat is designed to fit what the car manufacturer considers to be the average driver in terms of height, weight, and driving style. Thus the typical seat doesn't truly fit all drivers comfortably and it can cause excessive strain. The best-known seat manufacturers include Flofit and Recaro. The SLP Firehawk uses Recaro seats. Recaro, with their L Modular System seats, can custom-fit a seat to fit differing physiques and heights. This is done by combining four different seat cushions and three different seatbacks. As you would expect, you can order these seats in a variety of fabrics and leathers as well as having the seat covered in a fabric of your choice.

Recaro's ultimate seat is the CSE. It comes with electric seatback adjustment, electric air lumbar support, electric bi-level seat heating, power adjustable seatback side bolster supports, electrical height adjustment, an illuminated control panel located in the seat base, and there is also an optional three-position memory system.

Salvage yard scroungers should be on the lookout for Recaro-seat-equipped Trans Ams that were built from 1982 to 1984. The seats were part of the Special Edition Recaro Trans Am option.

Roll Bars

A roll bar is designed to protect the car's occupants in case the car rolls over, but it also has the benefit of reducing body and chassis flex. This is important in a road-race application. Roll bars are usually described as two-point, four-point, six-point, and so on. This refers to the number of places that it is bolted or welded on to the car's structure. The more points, the better as such a bar will form a protective cage around the driver and also provide more chassis rigidity. This is important for a race car, but it may be somewhat intrusive for normal use.

Roll bars are available from performance shops as kits, or you can take your car to a shop versed in race car fabrication and have a custom-made bar fitted to your Camaro or Firebird.

Finally, you should also consider installing a fire extinguisher, especially if you'll use your car in organized races. You may never have need to use one, but if you do, it could save you and your car. Dry chemical extinguishers are inexpensive, but the dry chemicals used can be difficult to clean up. For this reason you should consider a halon extinguisher which uses gas rather than chemicals, even though they are more expensive.

Chapter 14

Additional Modifications

There are a few other things that you can do to improve the performance of your 1982–92 Camaro or Firebird. Besides engine swaps, we'll take a look at some of the so-called "free" horsepower options that are available. Even if certain modifications yield only a small increase in power, the cumulative effect of several such modifications can make a considerable difference.

Underdrive Pulleys

One of the first modifications that anyone owning a 305/350 powered Camaro or Firebird should make is replace the stock pulleys with underdrive pulleys. This will reduce parasitic horsepower losses as the engine's accessories will be turning slower, resulting in about a 20hp increase. The pulleys that are usually replaced are those used on the alternator, crankshaft, and water pump. Owners who have installed mega-powered stereo systems are advised *not* to change the alternator pulley, however.

Steel pulleys will last longer than aluminum pulleys, so stay with the steel pulley for a street car.

By reducing parasitic losses, you can gain an easy 15–20hp by changing accessory pulleys. If you have a high-powered stereo system, leave the stock alternator pulley in place. Auto Specialties Inc.

Engine Swaps

There is no substitute for cubic inches—that's an old hot-rod saying and it still holds true today. More cubic inches mean more power. You can put practically any engine in the F-body engine compartment if you have the mind to do so. Still, there are some swaps that are a lot more practical and easier than others. In all cases, though, you should note that a swap will make your car illegal for street use under current EPA rules and regulations.

An obvious swap for 305 powered cars is the 350 engine. Save for cubic displacement, the engine is identical externally. There are many ways to go here. For example, you can purchase a 350 short-block from such sources as Performance Automotive Warehouse (PAW), or you can obtain the 5.7 liter HO engine from General Motors.

Two versions of the 5.7 liter HO "crate" engine are available from GM. The initial version of this engine, part number 10134338, in off-road trim puts out 345hp. It uses a four-bolt main cap block, forged steel crank with "pink" rods, 9.8:1 compression ratio hypereutectic pistons, a 0.480in lift hydraulic roller camshaft, Corvette 1.94x1.50in aluminum cylinder heads, HEI distributor, and an aluminum high-rise type intake manifold. There is also a street-legal version, part number 10185072, that can be swapped into LG4/L69 powered 305 F-bodies. It puts out 308hp.

SLP Engineering also offers complete engines. Starting with the 5.7 liter HO, the SLP 350 uses the T-Ram intake and puts out 350hp.

If you want more cubic inches from a 350, you may want to consider using a crank from a 400ci version of the small-block in the 350 block for 383ci. The 400ci crank is a cast unit but instead of using it, you should use SLP's 383 steel crankshaft. It has a 3.75in stroke, it is made from 5140 heat-treated forged steel, and it is manufactured with the same rear seal flange that 1987 and later small-blocks came with. You'll need new pistons, which SLP also has available.

Installation is a snap. All that is required is bolting off the old pulleys and installing the new ones. Use steel pulleys as they will outlast ones made from aluminum. SLP Engineering, Inc.

The basis for any increase in cubic displacement in the small-block is a stroker crank. Most often you'll find that the cast-iron crank from the 400ci small-block is used but *for extra durability, the same crank is available in forged steel from SLP Engineering. SLP Engineering, Inc.*

In terms of bore and stroke, many other variations have been accomplished by various engine builders, up to 454ci and more. Their practicality for a street engine is questionable, though. The F-body structure will need considerable bracing to handle the extra torque.

Another swap that you see from time to time is the 454 big-block engine. The engine fits surprisingly well in the F-body's engine compartment but its heavy weight exacts heavy penalties when it comes to handling, front tire wear, and rear tire traction. The big-block bolts right up to the stock small-block brackets and mounts, but Hooker's number 2226 headers are required along with additional modifications. The stock HEI distributor won't fit, so you'll have to use an older style distributor or an Accel small-cap unit, and you'll have to decide what kind of water pump and drive system to use. In addition, there is the question of which transmission to use

and most certainly, the rear will not be able to handle the 454's torque. When you go beyond the stock engine in terms of output, you'll also have to do something about the driveline—the stock T5 transmission and rear axle aren't up to the job.

Weight Reduction and Ballast

If you aren't in a position to add cubic inches to your engine, you can always reduce the weight that your engine has to push around—less weight means better acceleration. A word of caution is in order here: Some of the modifications suggested will affect the safety and street legality of your car. Lightening your car with fiberglass parts can affect the vehicle's crash worthiness. Likewise, the removal of antisway bars and the use of skinny pro-stock type wheels and tires will negatively affect handling. Some of these suggestions are effective only on a drag-racing car, and recommended only for a car used on the drag strip.

Here are some things you can do to reduce weight. Some are true no-cost (except for labor) modifications while others will set you back a few dollars.

Modification	Weight Savings (lb)
Remove front antisway bar	21
Move battery to trunk (weight transfer only)	0
Replace hood with fiberglass replica	18
Remove trunk pad sound deadener mat	22
Remove tailpipes from the muffler—on back	20
Remove rear fold-down seats	48

You can also get a complete short-block (or long-block, which includes cylinder heads) from GM and many aftermarket sources such as RHS. This is their street stock 350ci small-block which features a four-bolt block, forged crank, rods, and pistons, a Competition Cams camshaft, special oval-track type oil pan, and early style cylinder heads. With optional Dart II heads, the engine is said to put out 475hp. RHS Performance Engines

There are many aftermarket stroker kits available. This one is from Bill Mitchell and includes all the parts you'll need. Most likely, you'll need to have the reciprocating assembly rebalanced. Bill Mitchell Hardcore Products Inc.

Modification	Weight Savings (lb)
Replace front seats with pro-stock type seats	24
Remove rear antisway bar	14
Replace front wheels and tires with P165/15 tires and 15x3.5in aluminum wheels	32
Remove heater, stereo, speakers, under-carpet padding, center console, and miscellaneous interior items	68
Replace rear tires and wheels with drag slicks and 15x8.5in aluminum wheels	20
Remove spare tire, jack, and lug wrench	42
Remove exhaust system from header collector	56
Remove window crank mechanism, side window (replaced with plexiglass), and impact brace in doors	56
Replace cast-iron heads with aluminum heads	50
Replace cast-iron water pump with aluminum pump	8
Replace radiator with aluminum two-core radiator	15

Also remember that gasoline weighs 6.2lb per gallon and if you are drag racing, there is no need to run on a full tank. The total weight savings in the chart comes to 514lb, a substantial decrease—and with the exception of the cylinder heads, the cost is minimal. Removing weight does help improve acceleration.

The entire air intake for the radiator is from beneath the car on the Firebird. Once you modify your engine for more power, you'll have to increase airflow through the radiator and enlarge its capacity.

Although there is no weight saving in moving the battery to the trunk, the resulting transfer improves weight distribution by 1 percent, assuming the battery weighs about 30lb.

Cooling System

Whenever you modify an engine for more power, you'll also end up with more heat. On earlier Camaros and Firebirds this wasn't much of a problem—a more efficient fan and sometimes a larger radiator were all that was needed. Third-generation F-body engines run very hot from the factory for emission reasons, and because of their front end styling, radiator air is drawn from beneath the car. Third-generation Firebirds are more sensitive to overheating because there is no front opening as there is on Camaros. Because of the low air intake opening, it is a good idea to blow

If you have to change your water pump, replace it with a high-performance aluminum unit that has a maximum flow impeller. These are from Stewart Components. Stewart Components

There is no reason why you shouldn't use a synthetic motor oil. Besides the 10hp increase, you'll get superior wear protection, lower oil temperature, and extended change intervals. Mobil 1 has been around for a long time and is available in three grades—5W-30, 10W-30, and 15W-50.

A larger capacity oil pan ensures the oil pump pickup is always covered, especially during hard cornering. The Teflon-coated screen and the crankshaft wiper in the pan are designed to keep the oil from frothing and away from the rotating mass. Because there is less oil flying around in the oil pan to interfere and slow down the crankshaft, the result is a 5–10hp increase at 6000rpm. Hamburger's Oil Pans

out the radiator core of any dirt that may have accumulated on a regular basis.

To cure any overheating problems, you may have to install a larger radiator and larger electric fan. An aftermarket water pump may also be required. If you do install a higher performance water pump, make sure that your lower radiator hose is a noncollapsible design that has an inner spring.

It is generally agreed by performance tuners that you run a cooler than stock (195–205 degree) thermostat. For summer, use a 160 degree unit and for winter, a 180 degree unit. TPI Specialties also offer a 170 degree unit which they feel is the best way to go.

The internal combustion engine generates a lot of heat; the reason for this is because it isn't all that efficient. About 20 percent of the fuel energy is used to produce power and the rest of the heat energy produced must be dissipated elsewhere. Most of this heat originates in the combustion chamber. It must be dispersed to prevent thermal fatigue of the pistons, cylinder walls, and cylinder head. Depending on engine speed, up to 50 percent of the heat energy that is produced is dissipated through the radiator. At the same time, the combustion chamber must be kept cool enough to prevent pre-ignition and detonation.

Higher combustion chamber temperatures, which result in higher horsepower output, also require the use of higher octane fuel. Because fuels today are lower in octane than they were in the 1960s, today's engines aren't producing all the power they are capable of. And anything that stops or slows down the transfer of the excess heat produced in the combustion chambers will reduce engine efficiency.

Most people use a mixture of antifreeze (glycol) and water in their cooling system. What is not well known is that antifreeze *reduces* or slows down the transfer of heat generated in the combustion chambers to the coolant medium. Plain water has almost 2.5 times greater thermal conductivity than glycol-based coolants. Another way of saying this is that plain water is capable of transferring twice as much heat out of the system as compared to a 50:50 glycol mix.

Water also has a very high surface tension. In the cylinder head, especially under load, the heat produced is not evenly distributed to the metal. Instead, there are localized hot spots and it is through these spots that most of the heat is transferred to the coolant medium. However, at these hot spots the heat is so great that the water or antifreeze mix actually boils even though most of the cooling solution is below its boiling point. The culprit is the high surface tension of water, which makes it difficult to release the water vapor from the hot metal surface. The vapor bubbles on the metal surface create an insulating area, which slows down heat transfer.

This is where Red Line's WaterWetter comes in. WaterWetter reduces the surface tension of water by a factor of 2.0, resulting in much smaller water bubbles. This improves heat transfer on the localized hot spots by as much as 15 percent. Red Line performed tests to measure how quickly heat was removed from a 304 degree heated aluminum bar as it was quenched in different coolant combinations. All coolants were pressurized to 15psi and heated to 214 degrees. Water with WaterWetter required 3.2sec to reduce the temperature of the bar to 250 degrees; water alone took 3.7sec. A 50:50 mix and WaterWetter took 9sec; a 50:50 mix took 10.2sec while pure antifreeze took 21sec.

Using antifreeze will raise cylinder head temperature by about 1 degree F. for each percent of antifreeze mix used. Thus in the typical 50:50 mix you will see a cylinder head temperature increase of about 45 degrees. Not only will there be a power loss, but timing will have to be retarded or a higher octane fuel used to stop knocking.

Looking at it from another vantage point, using pure water with WaterWetter allows you to increase timing, which results in more power. Obviously this isn't a good idea in the northern areas of United States where temperature drops below freezing during winter.

But what about boiling over in summer? Besides protecting the engine against freezing, a 50:50 mix of antifreeze solution and water raises the boiling point to 265 degrees at 15psi while water alone boils at 250 degrees at 15psi. That isn't much of a difference, but you can raise the boiling point of water to 265 degrees by using a 23psi pressure cap. However, you may not need to.

Racers use WaterWetter and based on personal observation, water mixed with WaterWetter does

work. For best results, flush out the existing coolant mixture and fill the radiator with fresh water, adding the specified amount of WaterWetter.

Engine Oils

Often overlooked is the oil that is so vital to your engine. You can use a conventional oil and obtain good results as long as you change it every 2,000–2,500 miles but there is something better—synthetic oils.

Both synthetics and conventional oils do the same job of lubricating the engine's reciprocating parts and also acting as a coolant, removing heat from hot engine parts. Synthetics just do a much better job. Still, there is considerable apprehension regarding their reliability because synthetics earned a lousy reputation in the 1970s when a major refiner introduced a synthetic oil, Mobil 1. The formulation wasn't quite right and this resulted in numerous engine failures.

Today, the situation is much different. Synthetics are totally reliable and offer many advantages over conventional oils. For example, the 1992 Corvette left

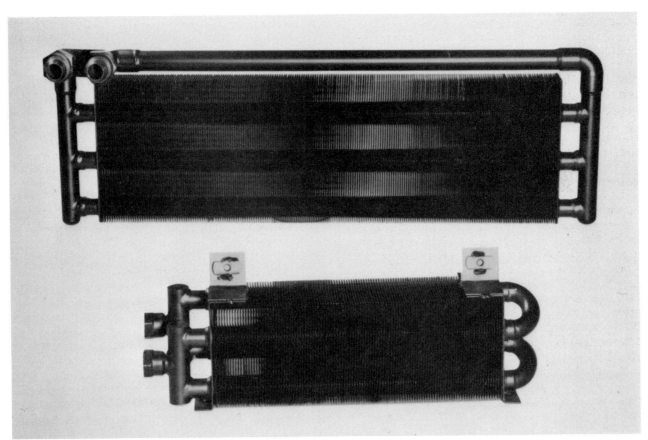

Keeping oil temperature down is just as important as keeping water temperature down to manageable levels. To do that, you'll need to install an auxiliary engine oil cooler. A well-designed oil cooler will reduce oil temperature by 30–35 degrees, however, a too low oil temperature *isn't advisable as it won't lubricate properly. Some oil coolers are thermostatically controlled and open only when oil temperature hits a predetermined temperature, usually around 180 degrees. Dunham-Bush Inc.*

the factory with synthetic oil. All Callaway Corvettes also specify the use of Mobil 1—any other oil will void the warranty. The best-known synthetics are Mobil 1, Red Line, and Amsoil. Valvoline, Pennzoil, and Castrol have also introduced synthetics.

Petroleum-based oils are a complex mixture of hydrocarbon compounds refined from crude oil. Through the refining process, most but not all of the contaminants that exist are removed. In addition, petroleum-based oils also contain wax, not known for its lubricating properties.

The base stock from which synthetics are made is free from contaminants and wax. Mobil 1's base stock is a compound of carbon and hydrogen molecules synthesized from ethylene gas molecules. Mobil calls this synthesized hydrocarbon fluid. Another synthesized fluid is added to this called organic ester.

Part of Red Line's base stock comes from vegetable oil sources and is modified to improve thermal stability, while other materials are added to complete the final product. Amsoil uses a combination of seven different base stocks in producing its final product.

Synthetic oils provide considerably higher viscosity ratings at critical areas without the use of viscosity improvers. A synthetic 10W-40 will generally have higher viscosity at high temperatures than a conventional 20W-50. The reason for this is the base stock from which the synthetic is constructed.

A major advantage of synthetics is their ability to remain stable at high temperatures without breaking down or oxidizing. Petroleum-based oils will boil away under high temperature. Depending on viscosity, they have a thermal breakdown between 350–400deg. This is an important factor because the upper cylinder area of an engine will see temperatures in the 600 degree range. Thus, a petroleum-based oil will begin to break down or oxidize almost immediately. Oxidation occurs when the hot oil is exposed to oxygen which then leads to the formation of organic acids which will combine and form varnish deposits. These deposits coat the metal, reducing the ability to transfer heat, and accelerating engine wear. Other by-products of oxidation include tar, sludge, and thickening.

Besides its resistance to viscosity loss at high temperatures, synthetics also have much stronger film strength. Film strength is the amount of pressure needed to force out a film of oil between two flat pieces of metal. A good petroleum-based oil measures at 500psi while most synthetics are around the 3,000psi level. Because of its inherent higher film strength, there is much less blow-by past the rings and thus less oil contamination.

While a petroleum-based oil will boil away as temperatures increase, a good synthetic such as Red Line will lose only about 4 percent of its weight. At higher temperatures, 475 degrees and above, conventional oils will volatize completely, while synthetics will still be lubricating at 700 degrees.

This probably is the reason why conventional oils have to be changed so often. Eventually, all the oil in the crankcase will oxidize and break down. The oil becomes saturated with contaminants, but contaminants that are the by-product of the oil's own decay and not totally due to contaminants produced by combustion. Synthetics don't need to be changed as often, but this is a point that elicits much skepticism.

Mobil used to advertise 25,000 mile change intervals, and even their current literature states 25,000. However, their position is that although the oil can go 25,000 miles, to ensure a margin of safety the oil can be changed sooner, depending on how the car is used. The same applies to Red Line. Red Line recommends oil changes between 12,000–18,000 miles, depending on the type of service and the degree of blow-by gas contamination. This means that with an older, looser engine, and if considerable stop-and-go driving is expected, oil drain intervals in the 10,000–12,000 mile range are recommended, with filter changes every 5,000 miles. New car owners should follow the manufacturer's warranty requirements.

Yet another benefit of synthetics is their ability to lower oil temperature in the crankcase. It is a well-known fact that oil does not only lubricate but also serves as a coolant medium, drawing heat away from the engine's reciprocating parts. However, as temperatures rise, petroleum-based oils have a tendency to bead on the metal surface while synthetics will wet the entire surface, showing affinity for the hot metal rather than itself. The lower oil temperature has the obvious effect of extending engine and oil life. Synthetics will reduce oil temperature by 20-30 degrees.

All this translates to better mileage because the oil is more "slippery," but more important is the increase in horsepower. A synthetic is good for a 5–10hp increase, as much as a set of "shorty" headers.

In addition to synthetics, also consider using an oil cooler. A good oil cooler will reduce oil temperature by 20 degrees, thereby extending oil life.

Finally, the LT1 engine as installed in the Corvette comes from the factory with synthetic motor oil. The 1993 Camaro and Firebird version of the LT1, however, does not. Yet, the Camaro and Firebird are equipped with an external engine oil cooler, while the Corvette isn't. According to General Motors, the reason for using conventional oil on the Camaro and Firebird was to reduce the cost of maintenance. Still, given the benefits of a synthetic, it is a worthwhile addition on any engine.

A deep-sump oil pan is a must on any performance engine. If you think about it, the 5qt capacity that is standard on the 305/350 may not be enough for high-performance use. When the engine is running, you have 1qt in the filter, another in the oil passages on the way to the bearings, and perhaps another on the way down to the oil pan. This doesn't include all

144

the oil that is thrashed up by the spinning crankshaft. That leaves about 2qt (or less) in the oil pan. Under hard acceleration or cornering, the oil pump pickup may become uncovered—and your engine won't run on air. Thus, a larger capacity oil pan is a worthwhile addition.

Performance Properties of Coolants

	Water & WaterWetter	50:50 Water/Antifreeze	70:30 Antifreeze/ Water Mix
Increase in cylinder head temperature	Baseline	+ 45deg. F.	+ 65deg. F.
Increase in octane (RON) requirement	Baseline	+ 3.5	+ 5.0
Change in spark timing to trace knock	Baseline	− 5.2 deg	− 7.5 deg
Change in torque	Baseline	− 2.1%	− 3.1%

Chapter 15

Specials

Unlike the archrival Mustang of which there are several aftermarket specials (such as the SAAC MK1, the Steeda GT, and the now-defunct Saleen), there hasn't been any serious attempt from an aftermarket supplier to produce a street-legal Camaro for the enthusiast.

There is, however, the Formula Firehawk, which is built by SLP Engineering, Inc. If you are interested in an impressive Firebird that has been modified and engineered for better acceleration and handling than the stock Firebird (or Camaro) that you can buy from your local dealer, this is the car for you. Actually, you can purchase the Firehawk from your local dealer under Special Order code RPO B4U.

The heart of the Firehawk is the emissions-legal 350ci V-8 which has been modified to produce 350hp. Similar to the GM 5.7 liter HO engine, it includes a high-flow TPI intake manifold, stainless steel tubular exhaust manifolds, and a special hydraulic roller camshaft. The cylinder heads are made of aluminum and use stainless steel valves.

As you would expect with such output, the entire stock driveline has been replaced. The stock transmission, whether it be automatic or manual, has been substituted with the ZF six-speed manual—the same unit that Corvettes use. The beefier Dana 44 rear axle houses a 3.54:1 axle ratio and has proven to be up to the task of handling the 390lb-ft of torque the 350 engine produces.

The Formula Firehawk is available from your local Pontiac dealer—just indicate Special Order code RPO B4U. It offers supercar performance, limited production, *and the advantage of a factory warranty.* SLP Engineering, Inc.

If you order the Competition Option, you'll get a Recaro driver's seat (passenger side optional), a six-point roll bar, a Simpson five-point harness, lightweight hood, rear seat delete, and the massive Brembo brakes. SLP Engineering, Inc.

The cast-aluminum wheels are made by Ronal and measure 17x9.5in front and rear. Tires are Firestone Firehawk SZs—P275/40ZR17. The brakes are the 1LE units. The Firehawk's springs, struts, and shocks are specially calibrated for a lower ride height and, as you would expect, great handling, with a 0.92 g skidpad figure on the full-tread street tires.

The only options currently available are driver's and passenger's Recaro seats and Simpson five-point seatbelt harnesses. There is also the Competition option which includes the 13x1.25in cross-drilled Brembo brakes, a Recaro driver's seat, the Simpson five-point harness, a lightweight hood, and a rear seat delete. At this writing, the Firehawk listed for $39,995, with the Competition Option going for an additional $9,995. Obviously this Firebird is not for everyone, and production was set at 250 units.

Performance is right up there: According to SLP, the Firehawk can reach 0-60mph in 4.6sec, the quarter mile in 13.2sec at 107mph, and at top speed of 160mph.

The Firehawk also sees action on the IMSA (International Motorsports Association) Firehawk series. SLP Engineering, Inc.

Sources

Suppliers

Accel Performance Products
P.O. Box 142
Branford, CT 06405-0142
Ignition and fuel injection components

Adaptive Technologies
127 N. Ventura Rd.
Port Hueneme, CA 93041
Multiple EPROM selection device

Addco Industries, Inc.
Watertower Rd.
Lake Park, FL 33403
Antisway bars, shocks, struts

American Best Car Parts Inc./Xenon
7400 Greenbush Ave.
North Hollywood, CA 91605
Aerodynamic bodystyling kits

American Industries Inc.
443 W. Alameda Dr.
Tempe, AZ 85282
Manufacturer of Cyclone, Thrush, Blackjack, Eagle
headers and exhaust systems

American Racing Equipment
17600 S. Santa Fe Ave.
Rancho Dominguez, CA 90221
Wheels

Arao Engineering Inc.
21400 Lassen St.
Chatsworth, CA 91311
Four-valve cylinder heads

Arizona Speed & Marine
Suite 100, 4221 E. Raymond
Phoenix, AZ 85040
Intake and exhaust systems

Auburn Gear Inc.
40 E. Auburn Dr.
Auburn, IN 46706
Differentials

Auto Avionics Instrument Research Inc.
P.O. Box 293
Monmouth Beach, NJ 07750
Gauges

Auto Meter Products Inc.
413 W. Elm St.
Sycamore, IL 60178
Gauges

Automotive Digital Systems
P.O. Box 348
Flint, TX 75762
Computer chips

Auto Specialties Inc.
13313 Redfish
Stafford, TX 77477
Underdrive pulleys

Autotronic Controls Corp.
1490 Henry Brennan Dr.
El Paso, TX 79936
MSD ignitions

B&M Automotive Products
9152 Independence Ave.
Chatsworth, CA 91311
Automatic transmissions and superchargers

Gale Banks Engineering
546 Duggan Ave.
Azusa, CA 91702
Turbochargers and engine components

Bell Tech
2882 E. California St.
Fresno, CA 93721
Suspension components

Borg-Warner
11045 Gage Ave.
Franklin Park, IL 60131
Transmissions, clutches

Borla Performance Industries
2639 Saddle Ave.
Oxnard, CA 93030
Exhaust systems

Brodix, Inc.
301 Maple
Mena, AR 71953
Cylinder heads

Art Carr Performance Transmission Products
10575 Bechler River Ave.
Fountain Valley, CA 92708
   Automatic transmissions

Carroll Supercharging
14 Doty Rd.
Haskell, NJ 07420
   Superchargers

Char-Trends
2677 McKelvey Rd.
Maryland Heights, MO 63043
   T5 transmission specialists

Classic Motorbooks, Inc.
729 Prospect Ave.
Osceola, WI 54020
   Automotive literature

Competition Cams, Inc.
3406 Democrat Rd.
Memphis, TN 38118
   Camshafts and valvetrain components

Compucar Nitrous Oxide Systems
509 Old Edgefield Rd.
North August, SC 29841
   Nitrous oxide systems

Crane Cams, Inc.
530 Fentress Blvd.
Daytona Beach, FL 32144
   Camshafts and valvetrain components

Crower Cams & Equipment Co.
3333 Main St.
Chula Vista, CA 91911
   Camshafts, valvetrain components, and connecting rods

Currie Enterprises
1480 N. Tustin Ave.
Anaheim, CA 92807
   Rear axles

Cuttler Systems
17525 144th Ave., Suite B
Spring Lake, MI 49456
   EFI components

Digital Fuel Injection
37732 Hills Tech Dr.
Farmington Hills, MI 48024
   Performance EFI systems and components

DynoMax
Div. of Walker Manufacturing
120 Michigan Blvd.
Racine, WI 53402
   Performance exhaust systems

Edelbrock Corp.
2700 California St.
Torrance, CA 90503
   Intake manifolds, carburetors, camshafts

Electromotive, Inc.
14004-J Willard Rd.
Chantilly, VA 22021
   Induction systems

Flowmaster Mufflers
2975 Dutton Ave., #3
Santa Rosa, CA 95407
   Mufflers

Fuel Injection Specialties
2238 Encino Loop
San Antonio, TX 78259
   Induction systems

Global West Suspension Components
1423 E. Philadelphia
Ontario, CA 91761
   Suspension components

Grant Products
700 Allen Ave.
Glendale, CA 91201
   Steering wheels

Guldstrand Engineering
11924 W. Jefferson Blvd.
Culver City, CA 90230
   Suspension components

Haltech: See ITAC

Harwood Industries Inc.
Rt. 3, Box 933 A
Tyler, TX 75705
   Fiberglass hoods

Headers By Ed, Inc.
2710-PS 16th Ave. S
Minneapolis, MN 55407
   Custom-made equal-length headers

Hedman Hedders
P.O. Box 2126
Culver City, CA 90232
   Exhaust headers

Holley Replacement Parts Division
11955 E. Nine Mile Rd.
Warren, MI 48089
   Carburetors and intake manifolds

Hooker Industries Inc.
1024 W. Brooks St.
Ontario, CA 91762
   Exhaust headers, roll bars

Hypertech
1910 Thomas Rd.
Memphis, TN 38134
   Computer chips

ITAC Automotive Technology
3121 Benton St.
Garland, TX 75042
   Haltech engine management systems

JFZ Engineered Products, Inc.
440 E. Easy St., Unit 3
Simi Valley, CA 93063
  Disc brake components

Kamei USA Auto Extras
P.O. Box 384
Northford, CT 06472
  Aero kits

Keiper Recaro Seating, Inc.
905 W. Maple Rd.
Clawson, MI 48017
  Recaro seats

Kenne-Bell Performance Products
10743 Bell Ct.
Rancho Cucamonga, CA 91730
  Ram air kits, filters, fuel injection components

Koni
8085 Production Ave.
Florence, KY 41024
  Shock absorbers and struts

Lee Power Steering
11661 Pendleton St.
Sun Valley, CA 91352
  Power steering units

Lingenfelter Performance Engineering
1557 Winchester Rd.
Decatur, IN 46733
  Performance engine components

M&H Tire Co.
77 Industrial Row
Gardner, MA 01440
  Tires

Manley Performance
13 Race St.
Bloomfield, NJ 07003
  Engine components

McLeod Industries
2906 E. Coronado St.
Anaheim, CA 92806
  Clutches

Midway Industries, Inc.
7171 Patterson Dr.
Garden Grove, CA 92641
  Centerforce clutches

Milodon Engineering
20716 Plummer St.
Chatsworth, CA 91311
  Deep-sump oil pans

Bill Mitchell Hardcore Products Inc.
80 Trade Zone Ct.
Ronkonkoma, NY 11779
  Engine components

Moroso Performance Products, Inc.
Carter Dr.
Guilford, CT 06437
  Oil pans, engine and driveline components

Art Morrison Enterprises Inc.
5301 8th St.
East Fife, WA 98424
  Suspension components

Moser Engineering Inc.
RR 4, Box 22 (Franklin Street)
Airport Industrial Park
Portland, IN 47371
  Axles, rear end components

Neat Top Company
P.O. Box 3205
Florissant, MO 63022
  Rear hatch replacements

Nitrous Oxide Systems (NOS)
5930 Lakeshore Dr.
Cypress, CA 90630
  Nitrous oxide systems

Offenhauser Sales Corp.
5232 Alhambra Ave.
Los Angeles, CA 90032
  Intake manifolds

Pacific Auto Accessories Inc.
5882 Machine Dr.
Huntington Beach, CA 92649
  Aerodynamic styling kits

Paxton Superchargers
929 Olympic Blvd.
Santa Monica, CA 90404
  Paxton superchargers

Powerhouse Products
127 N.W. 13th St.
Boca Raton, FL 33432
  O-ring groover

Rancho Suspension
P.O. Box 5429
6925 Atlantic Ave.
Long Beach, CA 90805
  Suspension components

Red Line Synthetic Oil Corp.
3450 Pacheco Blvd.
Martinez, CA 94553
  Synthetic oils and WaterWetter

Reider Racing
12351 Universal Dr.
Taylor, MI 48180
  Tremec manual transmissions

RHS Performance Engines
3410 Democrat
Memphis, TN 38118
  Reconditioned engines

Richmond Gear
Old Norris Rd.
P.O. Box 238
Liberty, SC 29657

SLP Engineering, Inc.
1501 Industrial Way N
Toms River, NJ 08755
 Engine, fuel injection, and driveline components

Splitfire, Inc.
Nine N. Broadway
Des Plaines, IL 60016
 Splitfire spark plugs

Stewart Components
1313 Temple Johnson Rd.
Loganville, GA 30249
 Water pumps

Stewart-Warner Instrument Corp.
1826 Diversey Pkwy.
Chicago, IL 60614
 Gauges

Street & Performance
Rt. 5, 1 Hot Rod Ln.
Hwy. 735 S
Mena, AZ 71953
 Performance components

Summers Brothers Inc.
530 S. Mountain Ave.
Ontario, CA 91762
 Driveline and engine components

Thrush Performance
2401 W. First St.
Tempe, AZ 85281
 Exhaust system components

Tilton Engineering Inc.
25 Easy St.
P.O. Box 1787
Buellton, CA 93427
 Racing clutches, starters, brakes

Total Seal Corp.
2225 W. Mountain View
Suite 6
Phoenix, AZ 85021
 Piston rings, engine and driveline parts

TPI Specialties, Inc.
4255 Co. Rd. 10 E
Chaska, MN 55318
 EFI, engine, and driveline components

Turbo Engineering
5601 S. Proctor Ave.
Tacoma, WA 98409
 Turbochargers

Turbo Technology
6229 S. Adams St.
Tacoma, WA 98409
 Turbochargers

Vortech Engineering
5351 Bonsau Ave.
Moorpark, CA 93021
 Superchargers

Watts Engineering
4115 S.E. 15th St.
Des Moines, IA 50320
 Rear-end specialists

Weiand Automotive
2316 San Fernando Rd.
Los Angeles, CA 90065
 Intake manifolds and blowers

Will-Burt Automotive
169 S. Main St.
Orrville, OH 44667
 Trick Flow cylinder heads

Mark Williams Enterprises, Inc.
765 S. Pierce Ave.
Louisville, CO 80027
 Driveline components

Wilwood Engineering
461 Calle San Pablo
Camarillo, CA 93012
 Disc brake kits

Wolverine Gear & Parts Co.
4790 Hudson Rd.
Osseo, MI 49266
 Camshafts and valvetrain components

World Products, Inc.
80 Trade Zone Court Bldg.
Ronkonkoma, NY 11779
 Dart cylinder heads

Darrell Young Racing Transmissions
7250 Hinds Ave.
North Hollywood, CA 91605
 Transmissions and components

Race Sanctioning Bodies
International Hot Rod Association (IHRA)
Box 3029
Bristol, TN 37625

International Motorsports Association (IMSA)
Box 10709
Tampa, FL 33679

National Association for Stock Car Automobile Racing
 (NASCAR)
Box K
Daytona Beach, FL 32015

National Hot Rod Association (NHRA)
Box 5555
2035 Financial Way
Glendora, CA 91740

Sports Car Club of America (SCCA)
9033 E. Easter Pl.
Englewood, CO 80112

Tuning and Rebuild Specifications

Capacities

Engine Year(s)/Type	Crankcase (qt)		Transmission (pt)			Axle (pt)	Cooling System (qt)
	W/Filter	WO/Filter	4-Spd.	5-Spd.	Auto.		
1982–86 2.5 liter	3.5	3	4.3	6.6	8.5	3.5	9
1982–89 2.8 liter	5	4	4.3	6.6	8.5	3.5	15
1989 3.8 liter Turbo	6	5	—	6.6	10	3.5	17
1990–92 3.1 liter	4.5	4		6.6	8	3.5	17
1982–92 5.0 liter	5	4	4.3	6.6	10	3.5	17
1986–92 5.7 liter	5	4	—	6.6	10	3.5	17

Note: Five-speed capacity is 5.5pt up to 1984. Automatic transmission capacity is 8.5pt for 1982.
Fuel Tank–All: 16.0gal

Crankshaft and Connecting Rod Specifications

1982–86 2.5 liter

Main bearing journal diameter	2.300in
Main bearing oil clearance	0.0005–0.0022in
Shaft end play	0.0035–0.0085in
Thrust	No. 5
Rod journal diameter	2.000in
Oil clearance	0.0005–0.0026in
Side clearance	0.0060–0.0120in

1982–89 2.8 liter V-6

Main bearing journal diameter	2.493–2.494in
Main bearing oil clearance	0.0017–0.0029in
Shaft end play	0.0019–0.0066in
Thrust	No. 3
Rod journal diameter	1.998–1.999in
Oil clearance	0.0014–0.0035in
Side clearance	0.0060–0.0170in

1990–92 3.1 liter V-6

Main bearing journal diameter	2.6473–2.6483in
Main bearing oil clearance	0.0012–0.0027in
Shaft end play	0.0002–0.0008in
Thrust	No. 3
Rod journal diameter	1.9983–1.9994in
Oil clearance	0.0013–0.0031in
Side clearance	0.014–0.027in

1989 3.8 liter

Main bearing journal diameter	2.4995in
Main bearing oil clearance	0.0003–0.0018in
Shaft end play	0.003–0.0110in
Thrust	No. 2
Rod journal diameter	2.487–2.495in
Oil clearance	0.0005–0.0026in
Side clearance	0.003–0.015in

1982–92 5.0 liter

Main bearing journal diameter	
No. 1	2.4484–2.4493in
No. 2–4	2.4481–2.4490in
No. 5	2.4479–2.4488in
Main bearing oil clearance	
No. 1	0.008–0.0020in
No. 2–4	0.0011–0.0023in
No. 5	0.0017–0.0032in
Shaft end play	0.0020–0.0060in
Thrust	No. 5
Rod journal diameter	2.098–2.099in
Oil clearance	0.0018–0.0039in
Side clearance	0.0080–0.0140in

1986–92 5.7 liter

Main bearing journal diameter	
No. 1	2.4484–2.4493 in
No. 2–4	2.4481–2.4490in
No. 5	2.4479–2.4488in
Main bearing oil clearance	0.0008–0.0020in
	0.0011–0.0023in
	0.0017–0.0032in
Shaft end play	0.0020–0.0060in
Thrust	No. 5
Rod journal diameter	2.098–2.099in
Oil clearance	0.0013–0.0035in
Side clearance	0.0060–0.0140in

Valve Specifications

1982–86 2.5 liter
Seat angle	46 deg
Face angle	45 deg
Spring pressure test	122–180lb @ 1.25in
Spring installed height	1.69in
Stem-to-guide clearance	
Intake	0.0010–0.0027in
Exhaust	0.0010–0.0027in
Stem diameter	
Intake	0.3418–0.3425in
Exhaust	0.3418–0.3425in

1982–89 2.8 liter
Seat angle	46 deg
Face angle	45 deg
Spring pressure test	194lb @ 1.18in
Spring installed height	1.57in
Stem-to-guide clearance	
Intake	0.0010–0.0027in
Exhaust	0.0010–0.0027in
Stem diameter	
Intake	0.3410–0.3420in
Exhaust	0.3410–0.3420in

1990–92 3.1 liter V-6
Seat angle	46 deg
Face angle	45 deg
Spring pressure test	215lb @ 1.291in
Spring installed height	1.575in
Stem-to-guide clearance	
Intake	0.0010–0.0027in
Exhaust	0.0010–0.0027in
Stem diameter	
Intake	0.3410–0.3420in
Exhaust	0.3410–0.3420in

1989 3.8 liter V-6
Seat angle	46 deg
Face angle	45 deg
Spring pressure test	185lb @ 1.20in
Spring installed height	1.73in
Stem-to-guide clearance	
Intake	0.0015–0.0035in
Exhaust	0.0015–0.0032in
Stem diameter	
Intake	0.3401–0.3412in
Exhaust	0.3405–0.3412in

1982–92 5.0, 5.7 liter V-8
Seat angle	45 deg
Face angle	45 deg
Spring pressure test	184–206lb @ 1.25in
Spring installed height	$1^{23}/_{32}$ (1988–92 exhaust $1^{19}/_{32}$)
Stem-to-guide clearance	
Intake	0.0010–0.0027in
Exhaust	0.0010–0.0027in
Stem diameter	
Intake	0.3410–0.3420in
Exhaust	0.3410–0.3420in

Piston and Ring Specifications

2.5 liter
Piston clearance	0.0014–0.0022in
Ring gap	
Top compression	0.10–0.020in
Bottom compression	0.10–0.027in
Oil control	0.015–0.055in
Ring side clearance	
Top compression	0.0015–0.0550in
Bottom compression	0.0015–0.0030in
Oil control	0.0010–0.0050in

2.8 liter
Piston clearance	0.017–0.043in
Ring gap	
Top compression	0.0098–0.0196in
Bottom compression	0.0098–0.0196in
Oil control	0.020–0.055in
Ring side clearance	
Top compression	0.0011–0.0027in
Bottom compression	0.0015–0.0037in
Oil control	0.0078in Max.

3.1 liter
Piston clearance	0.0022–0.0028in
Ring gap	
Top compression	0.010–0.020in
Bottom compression	0.010–0.020in
Oil control	0.010–0.050in
Ring side clearance	
Top compression	0.002–0.004in
Bottom compression	0.002–0.004in
Oil control	0.008in Max.

3.8 liter
Piston clearance	0.0008–0.0020in
Ring gap	
Top compression	0.10–0.020in
Bottom compression	0.10–0.020in
Oil control	0.015–0.055in
Ring side clearance	
Top compression	0.003–0.005in
Bottom compression	0.003–0.005in
Oil control	0.0035in Max.

5.0, 5.7 liter
Piston clearance	0.027in
Ring gap	
Top compression	0.10–0.020in
Bottom compression	0.10–0.025in
Oil control	0.015–0.055in
Ring side clearance	
Top compression	0.0012–0.0032in
Bottom compression	0.0012–0.0032in
Oil control	0.0020–0.0070in

Torque Specifications (lb-ft)

Engine Type	Cylinder* Head Bolts	Rod Bearing Bolts	Main Bearing Bolts	Crankshaft Pulley Bolt	Flywheel to Crankshaft Bolt
2.5 liter	85	32	70	160	44
2.8 liter	70	37	70	75	50
3.1 liter	33**	34–40	63–83	66–85	52 (auto.) 46 (man.)
3.8 liter	—***	45	100	219	60
5.0, 5.7 liter	60–75	42–47	70****	60	75

*Refer to manual for correct sequence.

**Rotate wrench an additional ¼ turn.

***Torque bolts initially to 25lb-ft, then turn an additional ¼ turn in two steps. If 60lb-ft is reached at any time, do not complete balance of ¼ turn.

****1985, 60–75lb-ft; 1986 inner 70–85lb-ft, outer 60–75 lb-ft; 1987–92, 63–85lb-ft.

Tune-Up Specifications

1982–84 2.5 liter
Spark plugs	R-44TS (R-44TSX w/TBI)
Gap	0.060in
Ignition timing	8B
Fuel pump	5.5-6.5psi (9.0–13.0psi w/TBI)
Idle speed	Man. 775rpm, Auto. 500rpm

1985–86 2.5 liter
Spark plugs	R-43TSX
Gap	0.060in
Ignition timing	8B
Fuel pump	9.0–13.0psi
Idle speed	Man. 775rpm, Auto. 500rpm

1982–84 2.8 liter
Spark plugs	R-43CTS
Gap	0.045in
Ignition timing	10B
Fuel pump	5.5–6.5psi
Idle speed	Man. 850rpm, Auto. 700rpm

1985–87 2.8 liter
Spark plugs	R-43CTS (R-43LTSE 1987)
Gap	0.045in
Ignition timing	10B
Fuel pump	6.0–7.5psi (9.0–13.0psi 1987)
Idle speed	Man. 600rpm, Auto. 500rpm

1988–89 2.8 liter
Spark plugs	R-43CTS
Gap	0.045in
Ignition timing	10B
Fuel pump	9.0–13.0psi
Idle speed	Man. 450rpm, Auto. 400rpm

1990–92 3.1 liter
Spark plugs	R-43LTSE
Gap	0.045in
Ignition timing	Refer to emissions sticker
Fuel pump	34.0–47.0psi
Idle speed	Refer to emissions sticker

1989 3.8 liter
Spark plugs	R-44TS
Gap	0.03544in
Ignition timing	See emissions sticker
Fuel pump	26–51psi
Idle speed	See emissions sticker

1982–84 5.0 liter V-8
Spark plugs	R-45TS
Gap	0.045in
Ignition timing	6B
Fuel pump	5.5–6.5psi (9.0–13.0psi w/TBI)
Idle speed	Man. 750rpm, Auto. 575rpm (475 w/TBI)

1985–86 5.0, 5.7 liter
Spark plugs	R-43CTS
Gap	0.045in
Ignition timing	6B
Fuel pump	9.0–13.0psi
Idle speed	Man. 750rpm (450 w/5.7 liter), Auto. 550rpm (400 w/5.7 liter)

1987–89 5.0, 5.7 liter
Spark plugs	R-42CTS (R-44TS 1987)
Gap	0.035in
Ignition timing	6B
Fuel pump	9.0–13.0psi
Idle speed	Man. 450rpm (500 w/1987 5.0 liter), Auto. 400rpm (500 w/1987 5.0 liter)

1990–92 5.0, 5.7 liter
Spark plugs	R-42CTS
Gap	0.035in
Ignition timing	6B
Fuel pump	9.0–13.0psi
Idle speed	Man. 500rpm, Auto. 500rpm

Firing Orders
5.0, 5.7 liter V-8
1-8-4-3-6-5-7-2
Distributor rotation: clockwise
Left bank: 1-3-5-7
Right bank: 2-4-6-8
3.8 liter V-6
1-6-5-4-3-2
Distributor rotation: none
Left bank: 1-3-5
Right bank: 2-4-6
2.8, 3.1 liter V-6
1-6-5-4-3-2
Distributor rotation: clockwise
Left bank: 1-3-5
Right bank: 2-4-6
2.5 liter
1-3-4-2
Distributor rotation: clockwise
Cylinder order: 1-2-3-4

GM Recommended TPI Fuel Pressures

Model Year/ Type	Pressure Rate (psi)
1985	34–40
1986	37–43
1987	37–43
1988	41–47
1989	41–47
1990	41–47
1990 LT5	48–55

Chart courtesy TPI Specialties, Inc.

Injector Flow Rates

Engine Type	Bosch Injector #	Pressure Rate
305	280-150-211	17lb/hr @ 40psi
350	280-150-223	22lb/hr @ 40psi
3.8 liter Buick GN	280-150-218	27lb/hr @ 40psi
3.8 liter Ford V-6*	280-150-756	32lb/hr @ 40psi

*Supercharged.
Chart courtesy TPI Specialties, Inc.

Horsepower Change at Varying Fuel Pressures

RPM	At 42PSI (stock) (hp)	At 46PSI (hp)	At 50.5PSI (hp)
2500	115.1	124.8	134.9
3000	135.4	158.9	174.5
3500	160.6	185.4	206.3
4000	190.7	212.0	227.0
4500	217.2	220.5	237.3
5000	216.7	214.2	226.4

Note: Engine is a stock 1987 305 with stock exhaust manifolds but without catalytic converter or muffler. The only modifications are TPI Specialties airfoil, spark plug wires, and TPI Specialties air filters and modified MAF sensor.

Chart courtesy TPI Specialties, Inc.

GM Performance Parts Small-Block V-8 Cylinder Head Availability

Part #	Description	Casting #	Material	Valve Diameters (in)
3987373	Service Repl.	3991492	Iron	2.02x1.60
464045	Service Repl.	462624	Iron	2.02x1.60
10134392	Bow Tie	14011034	Iron	2.02x1.60
10134336	Corvette	10088113	Aluminum	2.02x1.60
10051167	Phase 6 Bow Tie	14011049	Aluminum	2.02x1.60
10051101	Raised Runner Bow Tie	10051101	Aluminum	NA
25500141	Buick Stage II	25500141	Aluminum	2.10x1.625
10033867	Pontiac	10033867	Aluminum	2.10x1.625
10093328	Pontiac	10093328	Aluminum	2.16x1.60

Part #	Combustion Chamber Volume (cc)	Intake Runner Volume (cc)	Spark Plugs	Heat Riser Passage
3987373	64	157	Straight	Yes
464045	76	161	Straight	Yes
10134392	64	190	Angled	None
10134336	58	163	Angled	None
10051167	55	180	Angled	None
10051101	55	196	Angled	None
25500141	42	235	Angled	None
10033867	62	196	Angled	None
10093328	61	224	Angled	None

Chevrolet Small-Block Cylinder Head Airflow (cfm)

Cylinder Head Type	Intake Lift (in)					
	0.100	0.200	0.300	0.400	0.500	0.600
1987 stock 350, cast iron 083, 1.94x1.50in	44	101	155	182	196	202
1987 stock 350, cast iron 083, 1.94x1.50in, mild porting	58	115	165	191	202	208
Corvette 350 HO, aluminum 113, 1.94x1.50in	62	116	161	185	195	198
Corvette 350 HO, aluminum 113, 1.94x1.50in, mild porting	68	149	193	211	211	211
Stock 487, cast iron 1.94x1.50in	54	109	169	202	208	211
Stock 993, cast iron 1.94x1.50in	56	117	177	205	211	214
Stock 441, cast iron 1.94x1.50in	60	103	165	205	213	217
Corvette, aluminum 1.98x1.50in	70	130	182	215	230	236
Stock 492, cast iron 2.02x1.60in	56	120	179	217	232	238
Stock 492, cast iron 2.02x1.60in, ported	68	137	197	225	234	231
Bow Tie, cast iron 2.02x1.60in	61	127	185	224	233	236
Bow Tie, aluminum 2.02x1.60in, unported	61	123	179	214	226	229
Bow Tie, aluminum 2.02x1.60in	67	130	179	228	246	255
Bow Tie, aluminum 2.08x1.625in	56	125	193	237	264	273
Stock 487, cast iron 2.00x1.60in	67	131	193	217	228	233
Stock TS 441, cast iron 2.05x1.60in	71	141	191	230	233	233
Street Brodix 2.02x1.60in	70	138	185	218	224	221
Dart II 2.055x1.60in	76	136	191	227	248	261
Dart II 180cc runners, cast iron 2.02x1.60in, unported	60	113	175	208	223	229
Dart II 180cc runners, cast iron 2.02x1.60in, ported	80	143	205	252	244	249
Dart II, aluminum, unported	59	119	175	205	220	229
Dart II, aluminum, ported	68	145	202	226	235	238
Brodix #8, aluminum	62	122	172	223	241	252

Cylinder Head Type	Exhaust Lift (in)					
	0.100	0.200	0.300	0.400	0.500	0.600
1987 stock 350, cast iron 083, 1.94x1.50in	41	82	125	137	140	141
1987 stock 350, cast iron 083, 1.94x1.50in, mild porting	45	99	139	157	163	167
Corvette 350 HO, aluminum 113, 1.94x1.50in	49	98	130	152	159	156
Corvette 350 HO, aluminum 113, 1.94x1.50in, mild porting	47	99	138	163	177	185
Stock 487, cast iron 1.94x1.50in	43	80	113	134	144	148
Stock 993, cast iron 1.94x1.50in	47	88	122	140	146	148
Stock 441, cast iron 1.94x1.50 in	40	80	113	138	146	148
Corvette, aluminum 1.98x1.50in	61	118	162	181	181	188
Stock 492, cast iron 2.02x1.60in	58	103	140	163	175	183
Stock 492, cast iron 2.02x1.60in, ported	59	114	144	164	179	187
Bow Tie, cast iron 2.02x1.60in	55	113	145	165	171	171
Bow Tie, aluminum 2.02x1.60in, unported	54	103	130	148	157	161
Bow Tie, aluminum 2.02x1.60in	58	120	155	181	204	207
Bow Tie, aluminum 2.08x1.625in	63	115	154	181	195	203
Stock 487, cast iron 2.00x1.60in	60	113	148	173	187	196
Stock TS 441, cast iron 2.05x1.60in	60	114	151	175	191	203
Street Brodix 2.02x1.60in	64	121	155	187	200	204
Dart II 2.055x1.60in	65	123	174	184	191	197
Dart II 180cc runners, cast iron 2.02x1.60in, unported	49	103	124	138	144	148
Dart II 180cc runners, cast iron 2.02x1.60in, ported	68	118	156	177	190	196
Dart II, aluminum, unported	47	99	122	136	142	146
Dart II, aluminum, ported	58	115	155	173	183	190
Brodix #8, aluminum	49	103	142	175	202	211

Tests were performed at 28in of water on a Super Flow 300. Chart courtesy of TPI Specialties, Inc. On the Chevrolet tests, the three digits (i.e.: 083, 113, etc.) indicate the last three numbers of the head casting.

Tuned Port Injection System Manifold Runners & Base Specifications

Runner Type	Length (in)	Port (in)
Stock TPI	7.250	1.470 round
Lingenfelter/Accel	6.625	1.615 round
SLP cast runners	6.625	1.600 round
TPIS large tube	7.625	1.660 round
TPIS siamese large tube	7.625	1.660 round
Lingenfelter/Accel SuperRam*	4.125	1.870x1.970 "D" Shape
TPIS Mini-Ram*	3.500	2.600x1.350 entry 1.960x1.200 exit
Stock TPI manifold base	6.375	1.470 round entry 1.960x1.200 exit
TPIS Big Mouth base	6.125	1.750 round entry 2.090x1.280 exit
Lingenfelter/Accel SuperRam base	6.125	1.750 round entry 2.090x1.280 exit

* Runners only
Note: TPIS is TPI Specialties, Inc.

Stock Wheel Alignment Specifications

Note: P = Positive

1982–84
Caster (deg)
Range	2P–4P
Preferred setting	3P

Camber (deg)
Range	$3/16$P–$1^{13}/16$P
Preferred setting	1P

Toe-In (in)
Camaro	$7/32$P
Z-28	$5/32$P
Firebird	$1/16$P

1985
Caster (deg)
Camaro	
Range	$2^{1}/2$P–$3^{1}/2$P
Preferred setting	3P
Z-28	
Range	3P–4P
Preferred setting	4P
Firebird	
Range	$2^{5}/16$P–$3^{5}/16$P
Preferred setting	$2^{13}/16$P

Camber (deg)
Range	$1/2$P–$1^{1}/2$P
Preferred setting	1P

Toe-In (in)
Camaro	$5/32$P
Z-28	$1/16$P
Firebird	$1/16$P

1986
Caster (deg)
Camaro	
Range	$2^{1}/2$P–$3^{1}/2$P
Preferred setting	3P
Z-28	
Range	3P–4P
Preferred setting	4P
Firebird	
Range	3P–4P
Preferred setting	4P

Camber (deg)
Range	$1/2$P–$1^{1}/2$P
Preferred setting	1P

Toe-In (in)
Camaro	$5/32$P
Z-28	$5/32$P
Firebird	$1/16$P

1987–88
Caster (deg)
Range	$4^{1}/2$P–$5^{1}/2$P
Preferred setting	5P

Camber (deg)
Range	$1/2$P–$1^{1}/2$P
Preferred setting	1P (0, 1988)
Toe-In (in)	$3/64$P

1989–92
Caster (deg)
Range	$4^{3}/16$P–$5^{3}/16$P
Preferred setting	$4^{11}/16$P

Camber (deg)
Range	$3/16$N–$13/16$P
Preferred setting	$5/16$P
Toe-In (in)	0

Index